KV-373-957

Pearson Edexcel GCSE (9–1)

Spanish

Second Edition

Revision Guide

Series Consultant: Harry Smith

Author: Leanda Reeves

Also available to support your revision:

Revise GCSE Study Skills Guide   9781292318875

The **Revise GCSE Study Skills Guide** is full of tried-and-trusted hints and tips for how to learn more effectively. It gives you techniques to help you achieve your best – throughout your GCSE studies and beyond!

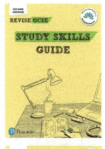

Revise GCSE Revision Planner   9781292318868

The **Revise GCSE Revision Planner** helps you to plan and organise your time, step-by-step, throughout your GCSE revision. Use this book and wall chart to mastermind your revision.

Difficulty scale

The scale next to each exam-style question tells you how difficult it is.

Some questions cover a range of difficulties.

The more of the scale that is shaded, the harder the question is.

 Some questions are Foundation level.

 Some questions are Higher level.

 Some questions are applicable to both levels.

For the full range of Pearson revision titles across KS2, 11+, KS3, GCSE, Functional Skills, AS/A Level and BTEC visit: www.pearsonschools.co.uk/revise

Contents

AUDIO

Audio files and transcripts for the listening exercises in this book can be accessed by using the QR codes throughout the book, or going to www.pearsonschools.co.uk/mflrevisionaudio.

Listen to the recording

A small bit of small print:
Pearson Edexcel publishes Sample Assessment Material and the Specification on its website. This is the official content and this book should be used in conjunction with it. The questions in Now try this have been written to help you practise every topic in the book. Remember: the real exam questions may not look like this.

Physical descriptions

Describe yourself and your friends successfully by using adjectives correctly.

Cómo soy

¿Cómo eres? — What do you look like?

Tengo el pelo / cabello … — I have … hair.

rubio y largo

castaño y rizado

negro y corto

Es pelirrojo/a. — He / She has red hair.

Tiene los ojos … — He / She has … eyes.
  azules / marrones / verdes. — blue / brown / green

Lleva gafas. — He / She wears glasses.

Es calvo. — He is bald.

Es gordo/a / delgado/a. — He / She is fat / slim.

Es guapo/a. — He / She is good-looking.

Soy alto/a / bajo/a. — I'm tall / short.

Tengo / Llevo barba / bigote. — I have a beard / moustache.

Tengo / Llevo un piercing. — I have a body piercing.

Adjectival agreement

Adjectives describe nouns. They must agree with the noun in gender (masculine or feminine) and number (singular or plural).

Grammar page 83

	Singular	Plural
Adjectives ending -o:		
Masculine	alt**o**	alt**os**
Feminine	alt**a**	alt**as**
Adjectives ending in a consonant:		
Masculine	azu**l**	azul**es**
Feminine	azu**l**	azul**es**

Remember: when you're describing hair and eyes, the adjectives need to agree with **pelo** and **ojos**, not with the gender of the person being described.

Quantifiers

Use **quantifiers** to extend your sentences and make them more interesting. Antonio and Pedro have used muy (very), bastante (quite) and un poco (a little). Quantifiers are positioned before the adjective and never change their endings.
Es bastante alta.   She is quite tall.

Worked example

Read the descriptions of four people.

Tengo los ojos marrones y el pelo negro. Soy un poco gordo. Mi amiga Elena es bastante alta y tiene el pelo muy corto y castaño. ¡Me encanta su cabello! **Antonio**

Tengo los ojos azules y el pelo rubio. No soy alto. Mi amiga Ana es bastante delgada. No lleva gafas y tiene unos piercings que no me gustan. **Pedro**

Complete the following sentences. Enter either **Antonio**, **Elena**, **Pedro** or **Ana**.

(a) ...Pedro... is short. **(1 mark)**

(b) ...Elena... has brown hair. **(1 mark)**

Pay attention to the gender of the adjectives used in these texts, so you know whether they are describing a boy or a girl.

Now try this

Read the texts from the worked example again. Complete the following sentences. Enter either **Antonio**, **Elena**, **Pedro** or **Ana**. You can use each person more than once.

(a) .... is not slim. **(1 mark)**

(b) .... does not wear glasses. **(1 mark)**

(c) .... dislikes the way their friend looks. **(1 mark)**

(d) .... has attractive short hair. **(1 mark)**

(e) .... has dark hair and eyes. **(1 mark)**

Character descriptions

Describe positive and negative aspects of personality using the verb ser.

¿Cómo es su personalidad?

Es ... He / She is ...

simpático/a	likeable
encantador/a	charming
hablador/a	chatty
leal	loyal
optimista	optimistic
razonable	reasonable

antipático/a	unpleasant
egoísta	selfish
perezoso/a	lazy
pesimista	pessimistic
tacaño/a	mean
travieso/a	naughty

 Soy simpática.
I'm friendly.

 Soy tonto.
I'm silly.

 Soy inteligente.
I'm intelligent.

 Soy serio.
I'm serious.

The verb ser (to be)

Grammar page 91

You need to be able to use ser in the present tense to describe characteristics.

Mi hermano es perezoso. My brother is lazy.

Mis primos son habladores. My cousins are chatty.

Aiming higher

Use a wider range of **vocabulary and verb forms** to create more complex sentences.

Mi compañero es bastante atrevido y yo soy muy valiente pero también somos responsables.

Try to mention some of these more interesting characteristics.

atrevido/a, fresco/a	daring, cheeky
celoso/a	jealous
comprensivo/a	understanding
engreído/a	conceited
equilibrado/a	well-balanced
loco/a	crazy
pedante, pretencioso/a	pretentious
responsable	reliable
sensible	sensitive
terco/a	stubborn
valiente	brave

Worked example

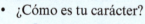

• ¿Cómo es tu carácter?

Soy bastante seria y muy simpática. A veces soy habladora pero nunca soy egoísta.

Aiming Higher

En mi opinión, soy bastante equilibrado y creo que también soy muy razonable. No obstante, no estoy muy seguro de mí mismo y puedo ser un poco tímido. Cuando era pequeño, era muy travieso y un poco tacaño con mis hermanos.

Remember to use the correct adjective endings. Here a girl is describing herself, and in the next paragraph it is a boy speaking.

Using exciting adjectives such as **equilibrado** and **razonable** makes this answer more interesting. By saying **puedo ser un poco tímido** (I can be a little shy) the student shows understanding of how to use infinitives. Also, talking about the past in **era muy travieso** demonstrates knowledge of the imperfect tense.

Now try this

Answer this question using at least three long sentences.

• ¿Cómo es tu personalidad?

Describing family

You often need to talk about your own family.

¿Cómo es tu familia?

Me parezco a mi hermano menor / mayor.
I look like my younger / older brother.
Me llevo bien con mis primos.
I get on well with my cousins.
Me llevo mal con mi hermanastra.
I don't get on well with my stepsister.

padre   abuelo   madre   abuela

hijo   hija

mi madrastra	my stepmother
mi padrastro	my stepfather
mi tío / tía	my uncle / aunt
su marido, su esposo	her husband
su mujer, su esposa	his wife

Possessive adjectives

Grammar page 84

Possessive adjectives agree with the noun they describe, not the person who 'possesses'.

	m.sing.	f.sing.	m.pl.	f.pl.
my	mi	mi	mis	mis
your (sing.)	tu	tu	tus	tus
his/her/its	su	su	sus	sus
our	nuestro	nuestra	nuestros	nuestras
your (pl.)	vuestro	vuestra	vuestros	vuestras
their	su	su	sus	sus

Mis padres están divorciados.
My parents are divorced.
Nuestros padres están separados.
Our parents are separated.
Sus padres están casados.
His/Her/Their parents are married.

Worked example

Escucha la entrevista con Carmen y pon una cruz ✗ en la respuesta correcta. **(1 mark)**

Según Carmen, es importante …

☒ **A** compartir cosas con tu familia
☐ **B** tener padres generosos
☐ **C** tener hermanos mayores
☐ **D** ver a sus padres cada día

Listen to the recording

– Para mí, pasar tiempo con tus parientes es importante.

Exam alert

When the multiple-choice questions are in Spanish, read them carefully and try to work out what they mean before you hear the recording. You may not remember that compartir means 'to share', but you can get the gist by understanding that con tu familia means 'with your family'.

To answer this question correctly, you need to know that parientes is a false friend: it means 'relatives', **not** 'parents'.

Now try this

Escucha la entrevista entera y pon una cruz ✗ en la respuesta correcta. **(1 mark)**

Carmen tiene una mala relación con …

☐ **A** su madre
☐ **B** su padre
☐ **C** sus parientes
☐ **D** sus hermanos

Listen to the recording

Remember to read all the options carefully before you listen.

Friends

You can use this page to prepare your thoughts about friends and friendship.

Los amigos

Un buen amigo debe ...	A good friend should ...
saber escuchar.	know how to listen.
ayudarte con tus problemas.	help you with your problems.
decir la verdad.	tell the truth.
estar siempre a tu lado.	always be by your side.
recordar tu cumpleaños.	remember your birthday.
ser como un hermano.	be like a brother.
aceptarte como eres.	accept you as you are.

Creo que los amigos son importantes.
I think friends are important.

Es importante que los amigos se lleven bien.
It's important that friends get on well.

Los amigos están ahí para apoyarte.
Friends are there to support you.

La amistad es más importante que el amor.
Friendship is more important than love.

The verbs deber and saber

deber – should	saber – to know (information)
debo	sé
debes	sabes
debe	sabe
debemos	sabemos
debéis	sabéis
deben	saben

Un buen amigo debería ser leal.
A good friend should be loyal.

Un buen amigo sabe guardar tus secretos.
A good friend knows how to keep your secrets.

Worked example

¿Cómo es un buen amigo?

En mi opinión, un buen amigo debe estar siempre a tu lado y sabe guardar tus secretos. Debe aceptarte como eres. Creo que los amigos son importantes.

Aiming Higher

En mi opinión, los amigos están ahí para apoyarte; no siempre están a tu lado pero pueden guardar tus secretos. Deben aceptarte como eres. Creo que los amigos son tan importantes como la familia. Es esencial que los amigos se lleven bien. A mi parecer, la amistad es más importante que el amor.

Opinion words (en mi opinión, creo que) can improve your communication and content.

Comparatives (es más importante que) show a confident use of more complex structures. Subjunctive clauses (se lleven bien after es esencial que ...) show more complex language handled confidently.

Exam alert

In the speaking exam, you can use the preparation time to make notes on what you want to say, but you mustn't prepare whole sentences and then just read them out.

Now try this

Answer the question in 30–40 seconds.
• ¿Cómo es un buen amigo?

Include **connectives** to make your work more coherent and fluent.

Role models

Can you describe what makes a good role model?

Los modelos a seguir

Un buen modelo a seguir es alguien que …
A good role model is someone who …

hace buenas acciones.	does good deeds.
inspira a otros.	inspires others.
apoya a organizaciones benéficas.	supports charities.
lucha contra la discriminación.	fights against discrimination.
ve el lado positivo de las cosas.	sees the positive in things.
cuida de los demás.	looks after other people.
tiene buenos modales.	has good manners.

Mi ídolo es mi profesor de educación física porque te apoya y nunca te juzga.
My idol is my PE teacher, as he always supports you and never judges you.

Verbs with prepositions

In Spanish many verbs need a preposition, which may or may not be the same as the English one.

cuidar de	to look after
depender de	to depend on
luchar por	to fight for
preocuparse de	to worry about
trabajar en	to work in

Sometimes the English verb does not need one but the Spanish does!

apoyar a	to support
ayudar a	to help

Use a variety of interesting verbs such as luchar or apoyar if you want to aim for a higher grade. Don't just stick with ser and tener!

Worked example

Explica lo que es un buen modelo a seguir.

(10 marks)

Aiming Higher

A mi modo de ver, un buen modelo a seguir es alguien que hace buenas acciones y sabe comunicarse bien. Mi inspiración es mi madre porque siempre ayuda a los demás. En mi opinión, los famosos no son buenos modelos a seguir ya que muchos no usan la fama de manera positiva y algunos son demasiado egoístas y arrogantes. En el futuro me gustaría ser un buen modelo a seguir para mis hermanos menores.

Aiming higher

This student has used a lot of exciting techniques to create a complex answer:
- ✓ unusual and interesting **vocabulary**
- ✓ long sentences using a variety of **connectives** (que, porque, ya que, y)
- ✓ justifications for the **opinions** expressed (porque siempre ayuda a los demás)
- ✓ a **negative** phrase (no usan la fama)
- ✓ an example of the **conditional tense** (me gustaría ser).

Now try this

Escribe un artículo para una revista sobre los modelos a seguir.
- Explica lo que es un buen modelo a seguir.
- ¿A quién admiras y por qué?

Escribe un texto de entre 50–60 palabras **en español**.

(10 marks)

Relationships

Be prepared to understand texts about relationships and to talk about them.

Las relaciones

¿Quieres salir el viernes?
Do you want to go out on Friday?

No puedo, estoy ocupado.
I can't, I'm busy.

Sí, podemos ir a la fiesta.
Yes, we can go to the party.

Conocí a mi novia en el instituto.
I met my girlfriend at school.

estar enamorado/a de — to be in love with
depender de — to depend on
contar con — to rely on
sentirse feliz — to feel happy

Rompí con mi novio.
I broke up with my boyfriend.

estar solo/a — to be alone
discutimos mucho — we argue a lot
a veces nos peleamos — sometimes we fight
sentimientos tristes — sad feelings

Radical-changing verbs

In radical-changing verbs, the vowel in the first syllable changes in the singular and third person plural.

Grammar page 88

	poder – to be able	querer – to want
I	puedo	quiero
you	puedes	quieres
he / she / it	puede	quiere
we	podemos	queremos
you	podéis	queréis
they	pueden	quieren

poder and querer are followed by the infinitive:
No puedo salir.   I can't go out.
¿Quiere ir al cine el viernes?   Does he want to go to the cinema on Friday?

Worked example

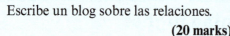

Escribe un blog sobre las relaciones.
(20 marks)

• ¿Te llevas bien con tu familia?
• ¿Por qué?

Me llevo bien con mi hermana porque es responsable y honesta, así que le puedo confiar mis secretos y nunca nos peleamos. Sin embargo, desde mi punto de vista, mi hermano pequeño es irritante y travieso, y nunca ayuda con las tareas en casa.

En general, tengo buenas relaciones con mi padre porque es muy comprensivo y puedo contar con él. Mi madre es estricta, así que discutimos a menudo, sobre todo cuando llego a casa muy tarde o cuando quiero llevar ropa que no le gusta. Por ejemplo, el fin de semana pasado, iba a una fiesta con mis amigas, pero mi madre me dijo que me tenía que cambiar de falda porque la que llevaba ¡era demasiado corta!

Exam alert

This can be a tricky topic. Try to:
• use phrases you know, but also use as much complex vocabulary as you can manage
• use a variety of tenses (this student has used the present, nunca nos peleamos, the imperfect, iba, and the perfect, mi madre me dijo)
• give opinions and explain or justify them.

Now try this

Escribe un artículo sobre el colegio para una revista. Escribe aproximadamente 80–90 palabras **en español**.
(20 marks)

• ¿Te llevas bien con tus compañeros de clase y con tus profes?
• ¿Por qué?
• Describe algo que haya pasado recientemente en el cole.
• Explica lo que quieres hacer el año que viene y por qué.

When I was younger

Use the imperfect tense to describe what you did when you were younger.

Cuando era pequeño

> Cuando era pequeño me gustaban los osos de peluche.

Cuando era pequeño ...	When I was younger ...
me encantaba explorar.	I loved exploring.
me chiflaban los dibujos animados.	I loved cartoons.
jugaba en mi habitación.	I used to play in my room.
comía caramelos.	I ate sweets.
bebía más leche.	I drank more milk.
montaba en bici por el parque.	I rode my bike in the park.
me subía a los árboles.	I climbed trees.
era tan inocente.	I was so innocent.
no era travieso/a.	I wasn't naughty.
Cuando éramos pequeños ...	When we were little ...
mi familia y yo comíamos juntos.	my family and I ate together.
leíamos muchos tebeos.	we read lots of comics.
jugábamos al ajedrez.	we played chess.
queríamos ser mayores.	we wanted to be grown-up.
nunca nos aburríamos.	we were never bored.

Imperfect tense

> Grammar page 94

The imperfect tense is used to describe what **used to happen** or what **was happening**.
It is formed as follows:

hablar to speak	comer to eat	vivir to live
hablaba	comía	vivía
hablabas	comías	vivías
hablaba	comía	vivía
hablábamos	comíamos	vivíamos
hablabais	comíais	vivíais
hablaban	comían	vivían

> Use these **time expressions** to add detail to sentences you write with the imperfect tense.
> A menudo nos reuníamos.
> We **often** got together.
> Mi padre siempre cocinaba.
> My dad **always** used to cook.
> Nunca arreglaba mi habitación.
> I **never** tidied my room.
> A veces cantaba canciones pop con mis amigos.
> **Sometimes** I would sing pop songs with my friends.

Worked example

An actor is talking about his childhood. Listen and answer the following question **in English**.
What was good about his family?   **(1 mark)**

His sisters loved doing the same things as him.

Listen to the recording

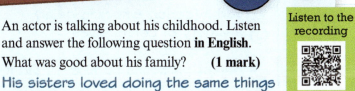

– Cuando era pequeño era muy travieso. Tenía dos hermanas igual de traviesas y nos encantaba hacer las mismas cosas.

> The text begins in the imperfect tense (Cuando era pequeño), so you know the man is describing his past experiences.
> The question asks you about his family, so you should be listening out for any family members, not just the word familia. He talks about his sisters (hermanas).
> When the question asks about a positive aspect of something, remember to listen out for any opinions mentioned. He says nos encantaba.

Now try this

Listen to the whole recording from the worked example and answer the following questions **in English**.

Listen to the recording

(a) Why is the garden mentioned?   **(1 mark)**

(b) What did they use to do before going to bed?   **(1 mark)**

Peer group pressure

Use the language here to help you write about peer group influences.

La presión del grupo

Puede ser una influencia positiva o negativa.
It can be a positive or negative influence.

Gracias a mis amigos …	Thanks to my friends …
empecé a estudiar más.	I began to study more.
dejé de beber.	I stopped drinking.
resistí las tentaciones.	I resisted temptations.
hice más deporte.	I did more sport.
comencé a comer de un modo más sano.	I started to eat more healthily.
tomé mis propias decisiones.	I made my own decisions.

Cedió ante la presión del grupo.
He / She gave in to peer pressure.

Tomó drogas.	He / She took drugs.
Probó un cigarrillo.	He / She tried a cigarette.
Fumó.	He / She smoked.
Bebió alcohol.	He / She drank alcohol.
Tomó malas decisiones.	He / She made bad decisions.

Preterite tense

Grammar page 93

To form the preterite tense of regular verbs, replace the infinitive ending as follows:

	hablar to speak	comer to eat	vivir to live
I	hablé	comí	viví
you	hablaste	comiste	viviste
he / she / it	habló	comió	vivió
we	hablamos	comimos	vivimos
you	hablasteis	comisteis	vivisteis
they	hablaron	comieron	vivieron

Be careful with accents!
hablo – I speak
BUT habló – he / she spoke

Worked example

Escribe de

- tus experiencias de presión del grupo. **(5 marks)**

Aiming Higher

El mes pasado cedí ante la presión del grupo y empecé a fumar cigarrillos. Lo hice para ser aceptado pero en realidad lo odiaba. Es una estupidez y esta semana dejé de fumar porque no quiero caer en el hábito de fumar cada día como algunos de mis amigos. A partir de ahora, intentaré tomar mis propias decisiones.

Aiming higher

Try to include the following features in your writing:
- ✓ a range of tenses (present, preterite, imperfect, future)
- ✓ a good number of less common verbs (ceder, empezar, dejar)
- ✓ a variety of connectives (y, pero, como)
- ✓ object pronouns (lo hice – I did it).

Now try this

Escribe un artículo sobre la amistad. **Debes** incluir los puntos siguientes:

- describe a un/a amigo/a
- explica lo que es un buen amigo / una buena amiga
- tus experiencias recientes de presión del grupo
- los planes para el futuro que tenéis tú y este/a amigo/a.

Escribe aproximadamente 80–90 palabras **en español**.

(20 marks)

Customs

Make sure you can understand different types of texts about Spanish culture.

Las costumbres españolas

España es un país de costumbres.
Spain is a country with lots of customs.
Los españoles suelen ... Spanish people tend to ...

ir de tapas / tapear.	go out to eat tapas.
tomar una siesta.	take a nap (traditionally after lunch).
salir a tomar algo en las terrazas.	go out to cafés with terraces.
pasear.	go for a stroll.

comer las doce uvas en Nochevieja.
eat the twelve grapes for New Year's Eve (one on each stroke of midnight).

saludar a la gente con dos besos.
greet people with two kisses.

ir a la costa en verano.
go to the coast in summer.

comer más tarde que otros europeos.
eat later than other Europeans.

Muchos españoles se acuestan tarde.
Many Spanish people go to bed late.

Los horarios de las tiendas son más amplios que en otros países.
Shop opening hours are longer than in other countries.

Special calendar dates

Learn these special days in Spanish.

la Nochebuena	Christmas Eve
la Navidad	Christmas
la Cuaresma	Lent
la Pascua / la Semana Santa	Easter / Holy Week
el Viernes Santo	Good Friday
el Lunes de Pascua	Easter Monday
¡Feliz cumpleaños!	Happy birthday!
¡Feliz Año Nuevo!	Happy New Year!

¡Feliz Navidad!
Happy Christmas!

The seasons

el otoño	autumn
la primavera	spring
el verano	summer
el invierno	winter

Worked example

  LISTENING TRACK 5

You are listening to a radio programme about customs in Spain. Answer the following question **in English**.

What **two** benefits are said to result from the custom discussed? **(2 marks)**

improves your health and helps you avoid stress

 Listen to the recording

– Vamos a hablar de las costumbres de aquí. ¿Qué opinas de la siesta?

– Es cierto que la siesta forma parte de nuestras tradiciones desde hace mucho tiempo. Además, se dice que mejora la salud y que ayuda a evitar el estrés.

Listening strategies

When you are listening to a conversation, pay particular attention to the questions, as they will guide you to the information you need to complete the task successfully.

Here you need to understand that **mejora la salud** means 'improves your health'. Even if you didn't recognise the verb **mejorar**, you could make the link to the word **mejor**, meaning 'better'.
El estrés is a cognate that is easy to pick out. If you don't remember the verb **evitar**, you can make a sensible guess that it would help avoid stress.

Now try this

   LISTENING TRACK 6

Now listen to the rest of the programme from the worked example. Answer the following questions **in English**.

(i) Where has this tradition been lost? **(1 mark)**

(ii) What has been proved in the past by scientific studies? **(1 mark)**

 Listen to the recording

Everyday life

Use a variety of verbs to talk or write about your everyday activities.

La vida cotidiana

¿Qué haces durante la semana?
What do you do during the week?
Me despierto a las seis y media.
I wake up at 6.30.
Me ducho deprisa.   I shower quickly.
Me lavo los dientes.   I brush my teeth.
Desayuno.   I have breakfast.
Salgo de casa.   I leave the house.
Voy al instituto en autobús.
I go to school by bus.
Vuelvo a casa.   I return home.
Hago los deberes.   I do my homework.
Ceno temprano.   I have dinner early.
Me duermo a las diez. I go to sleep at
                           10 o'clock.

¿Qué haces los fines de semana?
What do you do at weekends?
Me levanto tarde.   I get up late.
Desayuno a las once y media.
I have breakfast at 11.30.
Me baño y me visto.
I have a bath and get dressed.
Hago deporte.   I do sport.
Veo la tele.   I watch TV.
Descanso en mi habitación.
I relax in my room.
Almuerzo con mi familia.
I have lunch with my family.
Salgo con mis amigos.
I go out with my friends.
Me acuesto muy tarde.   I go to bed very late.

> Remember: reflexive verbs have a **pronoun** before the verb: **Me** levanto.   I get up.

Talking about time

Son …   It's …
A …   At …

las dos y
media

las tres
menos cuarto

las tres
menos diez

> Note the exception:
> Es la una. A la una.
> It's one o'clock.
> At one o'clock.

Worked example

Escribe sobre tu rutina diaria en casa.   **(5 marks)**

> Normalmente me despierto temprano, a las seis, pero ayer me levanté a las siete porque estaba cansado.

Aiming Higher

> Mis padres se despiertan a las seis. Siempre me ducho, pero mi hermano se baña. Pasa demasiado tiempo en el cuarto de baño. ¡Ayer pasó treinta minutos! ¡Ojalá tuviera mi propio cuarto de baño!

Time references and adverbs

When talking about everyday life, it is important to use time references and adverbs to add detail to your sentences.

todos los días / cada día every day
de vez en cuando   from time to time
a menudo   often
siempre   always

> • This version has added extra information, with his opinion of his brother's behaviour (**pasa demasiado tiempo en el cuarto de baño**).
> • It also deserves a higher grade as it includes a **complex structure** (**ojalá tuviera**) to say he wishes he had his own bathroom.

Now try this

Tu amiga Ana va a visitarte a Inglaterra. Escribe un correo electrónico. **Debes** incluir los puntos siguientes:

• tu rutina diaria en casa
• lo que hiciste el fin de semana pasado

• los planes que tienes para la visita de Ana.

Escribe aproximadamente 80–90 palabras **en español**.

(20 marks)

Meals at home

Eating at home is an important topic. This page will help you talk and write about it.

Las comidas en casa

el desayuno	breakfast
el almuerzo / la comida	lunch
la merienda	afternoon snack
la cena	dinner
Es importante …	It's important …
comer juntos.	to eat together.
sentarse a la mesa.	to sit down at the table.
compartir experiencias.	to share experiences.

Desayunamos cereales y fruta.
We have cereal and fruit for breakfast.

Nos gusta comer pollo asado.
We like to eat roast chicken.

Las chuletas de cerdo son deliciosas.
Pork chops are delicious.

la carne picada	mince
los fideos	noodles
las verduras	vegetables
los huevos fritos	fried eggs
el filete muy hecho	steak well done

To say how long you have been doing something

Use desde hace + present tense **or** llevo + the gerund:

Grammar page 92

Como alimentos ecológicos desde hace dos años.
I have been eating organic food for two years.

Llevo cinco meses comiendo pescado fresco.
I have been eating fresh fish for five months.

To say you have just done something

Use acabo de + infinitive:
Acabo de volver de Italia.
I have just returned from Italy.

Worked example

Read the article below.

Las comidas en casa

Hoy en día parece que nadie tiene tiempo para nada, todos corremos de un sitio a otro, de un momento a otro. Desde hace unos años las familias tienen cada vez menos tiempo de sentarse a la mesa para comer juntos. De hecho, la comida sabe mejor porque se comparte el momento y las anécdotas familiares. Comer juntos también ayuda a la comunicación entre padres e hijos. A veces es difícil lograrlo, para ello se necesita organización. Acabo de cenar con mis vecinos y en su casa los niños aprenden a interesarse por el resto de la familia.

Answer the following question **in English**.
What has decreased in the last few years? **(1 mark)**
time spent eating together as a family

Learning vocabulary

To prepare for your exam, you need to learn lots of vocabulary.
- ✓ **Look** at the words and memorise them.
- ✓ **Cover** the words.
- ✓ **Write** the words.
- ✓ **Look** again.
- ✓ **See** how many you got right.

Start by covering the English words. When you're confident, cover the Spanish words and see if you can remember them from the English prompts.

Remember that you do not need to answer in full sentences.

Now try this

Read the article in the worked example again. Answer the following questions **in English**.
(a) What effect does eating together have on food? **(1 mark)**
(b) How can you overcome difficulties over eating together? **(1 mark)**
(c) What do children learn from eating with adults? **(1 mark)**

Food and drink

Make sure you revise food and drink words carefully, as there are not many cognates to help you!

Ir de tapas

Me gusta ir de tapas.	I like to go out for tapas.
la carne fría cortada en lonchas	cold sliced meat
la tortilla de patatas	potato omelette
las albóndigas	meatballs
el pincho / la brocheta	kebab
el queso (de cabra)	(goat's) cheese
el pescado	fish
el arroz	rice
la ensalada mixta	mixed salad
los pimientos cocidos	roasted peppers
los mariscos	seafood
los panecillos	bread rolls
la cerveza	el zumo de fruta
el agua mineral	el vino
el refresco	

Articles: 'the', 'a' and 'some'

There are four different ways to say 'the' in Spanish.

Grammar page 82

	Singular	Plural
Masculine	el atún	los espaguetis
Feminine	la sopa	las salchichas

There are two ways to say 'a', plus two plural forms, which mean 'some'.

	Singular	Plural
Masculine	un bocadillo — a sandwich	unos bocadillos — some sandwiches
Feminine	una loncha — a slice	unas lonchas — some slices

Exam alert

In the role play section of the speaking exam, make sure you pay attention to the register you must use – tú or usted. Remember to use the correct verb endings when asking questions.

Worked example

You are in a restaurant in Spain. The teacher will play the part of the waiter/waitress and will speak first.

Usted está en un restaurante de España.

1. Bebida – descripción
   ¿En qué puedo servirle?
   Me gustaría tomar un zumo de fruta.
2. Comida española – razón
   Muy bien. ¿Le gusta la comida española?
   Me encanta la comida española porque es muy variada y deliciosa.
3. !
   Sí, claro. Habla muy bien el español. ¿De dónde es?
   Gracias. Soy inglesa.
4. Planes – hoy
   ¿Qué planes tiene para hoy?
   Voy a hacer una excursión en bici.
   Muy bien.
5. ? Menú del día
   ¿Tiene una pregunta?
   ¿Hay menú del día?
   Claro que sí.

Exam alert

For the Foundation tier, you will need to ask a question, shown by ?. In the Higher tier role play, there are TWO questions for you to ask. Both Foundation and Higher role plays include a response to something you have not prepared, shown by !. Here the unexpected question is ¿De dónde es? and the candidate answers by giving his/her nationality.

Be prepared in a role play to answer questions or give opinions on a range of topics. For example, here the role play is set in a restaurant but you also have to say your nationality and give your opinion about Spanish food.

The unexpected question is ¿Y para beber? Can you think of any other questions you could have been asked here?

Now try this

Prepare your own answers to the following restaurant role play prompts. Then listen to the audio recording of the teacher's part and fill in your answers in the pauses.

1. Mesa – número de personas
2. Comida – descripción
3. !
4. Comida – opinión
5. ? Precio – comida

Listen to the recording

Shopping for clothes

Use the language here to give your opinion about shopping.

Ir de compras

Me chifla ir de compras.
I love going shopping.

Odio los grandes almacenes.
I hate department stores.

Me encantan las tiendas pequeñas.
I love small shops.

No me gustan nada los centros comerciales.
I really don't like shopping centres.

el escaparate	the shop window
el probador	the changing room
la ropa	clothes
los guantes	gloves
los vaqueros	jeans
las joyas	jewellery
el brazalete / la pulsera	bracelet
las zapatillas de deporte	trainers

Mi número de zapato es el 42.
My shoe size is 42.

Busco un vestido de talla 38.
I am looking for a size 38 dress.

Direct object pronouns

	Masculine	Feminine
it	lo	la
them	los	las

Grammar page 87

– Estos zapatos son demasiado pequeños.
– Lo siento, no los tengo en su número.

Aiming higher

Try to use direct object pronouns in your spoken and written Spanish to create more complex statements.

Odio usar los probadores pero es difícil evitarlos en las tiendas de ropa.
I hate using changing rooms but it's hard to avoid them in clothes shops.

Lee el artículo sobre comprar por Internet.

> Las ventajas de comprar por Internet son claras: se evita hacer colas y también con solo hacer clic se puede comprar artículos que no se encuentran en tu país. Pero comprar por Internet también tiene sus desventajas. Algunas de ellas son los pagos, la devolución de los artículos y el ser víctima de fraude. A pesar de todo esto, es posible que en un futuro no muy lejano la mayoría de nuestras compras se hagan de esta forma. Lo importante es que los consumidores tengan tanto cuidado en el mundo virtual como en el mundo real.

Answer the question in English.

Mention **two** advantages of buying online.

avoiding queues / finding items not in your country

Pon una cruz ✗ en la casilla correcta.
Una de las ventajas de comprar por Internet …

(1 mark)

☐ **A** no existe
☐ **B** es la seguridad
☐ **C** son los precios
☒ **D** es encontrar artículos del extranjero

The key to knowing that D is correct is understanding the phrase **comprar artículos que no se encuentran en tu país**. Make sure you learn as much higher-level vocabulary as possible.

Lee el artículo otra vez. Pon una cruz ✗ en la casilla correcta.

Según el artículo, dentro de poco mucha gente …

(1 mark)

☐ **A** visitará más tiendas virtuales
☐ **B** gastará más dinero en los centros comerciales
☐ **C** tendrá problemas comprando en el mundo virtual
☐ **D** no querrá hacer compras por Internet

Social media

This page gives you information about social media to help with listening and reading tasks.

Las redes sociales

Uso las redes sociales para …
I use social media to …

intercambiar información personal.
exchange personal information.

compartir fotos y vídeos.
share photos and videoclips.

conocer a nueva gente. meet new people.

organizar las salidas arrange to meet
con mis amigos. up with my friends.

chatear en línea. chat online.

mandar mensajes a mi novio/a.
send messages to my boyfriend/girlfriend.

escribir blogs. write blogs.

Para usarlas con seguridad hay que …
To use it safely you should …

proteger la información personal.
protect your personal information.

No hay que … You should not …

compartir las claves / contraseñas.
share your passwords.

abrir mensajes o ficheros extraños.
open strange messages or files.

Cognates

✓ Look out for cognates in Spanish. These are words that **resemble**, or are the **same as**, words in English, e.g.

mensaje message
fotos photos

✓ Look out for ways to **connect** Spanish words too. This will help you work out the meaning of new words and help you remember vocabulary, e.g.

flor	flower	floristería	florist's
libro	book	librería	bookshop
pan	bread	panadería	bakery
seguro/a	safe	seguridad	safety
un intercambio	an exchange		
intercambiar	to exchange		
una ficha	file (made of card)		
un fichero	(computer) file		

Worked example

Olivia has recorded a podcast about social media. Put a cross ✗ in the correct box. **(1 mark)**

Olivia thinks that social media …
- ☐ **A** is dangerous for adolescents
- ☐ **B** needs more safety measures
- ☒ **C** is good for sharing photos
- ☐ **D** is less popular now

Listen to the recording

– En mi opinión, las redes sociales no son peligrosas si vas con cuidado. Las uso porque es fácil compartir fotos con mis amigos.

Listening strategies

Remember to read the statements **before** you begin listening and to predict the types of words or phrases you may hear. While listening and before choosing your answer, think carefully about the **context** of any relevant vocabulary you heard.

The word for 'dangerous' (option A) is mentioned, but in a negative statement: **no son peligrosas si vas con cuidado.** The key to understanding the context and choosing option C is the phrase **es fácil**, which equates to 'is good for … '.

Now try this

Listen to the whole podcast from the worked example and put a cross ✗ in the correct box. **(1 mark)**

Olivia is most impressed with how social media …
- ☐ **A** can block offensive users
- ☐ **B** allows international communication
- ☐ **C** helps her to arrange meetings
- ☐ **D** helps users maintain privacy

Listen to the recording

Technology

Technology is part of our everyday life. Make sure you can talk about it in Spanish.

La tecnología

la Xbox
el ordenador
los videojuegos
los altavoces
los auriculares
la tableta
el móvil

Usamos la tecnología todos los días

Estamos en contacto con nuestras familias.
We contact our families.
Descargamos MP3/aplicaciones.
We download MP3s/apps.
Subimos vídeos.   We upload videoclips.
Mandamos mensajes (de texto).
We send text messages.
Respondemos a los correos electrónicos.
We reply to emails.
Imprimimos los deberes.
We print our homework.
Grabamos discos.   We burn disks.
Escribimos a máquina.   We type.

Aiming higher

Use interesting adjectives to describe technology and other topics. Stay clear of over-used adjectives like interesante, divertido or aburrido.

adecuado/a	suitable
breve	brief
flexible	flexible
gratis	free
necesario/a	necessary
nuevo/a	new
numeroso/a	numerous
peligroso/a	dangerous
práctico/a	practical
rápido/a	fast

Worked example

Read the opinions about technology.
Complete the following sentence. Enter either **Gabriela, Pablo, Mateo** or **Nuria**.
Gabriela does not like sending texts. **(1 mark)**

> Remember that there are a number of ways to express a negative opinion. Pablo does not say **no me gusta** but instead says **es aburrido** to express dislike.

Gabriela: Uso el móvil cada día y siempre descargo canciones nuevas pero creo que es aburrido mandar mensajes de texto.

Pablo: No me interesan los ordenadores porque los encuentro peligrosos, así que en mi tiempo libre prefiero hacer otras cosas.

Mateo: Lo que más me gusta de la tecnología es que la mayoría de las aplicaciones que uso son gratis.

Nuria: Todos mis amigos usan tabletas u ordenadores para jugar a juegos pero no son fáciles. Por eso solo uso el ordenador para hacer e imprimir los deberes.

Now try this

Read the texts from the worked example again and complete the following sentences. Enter either **Gabriela, Pablo, Mateo** or **Nuria**. You can use each person more than once.

(a) .... finds computer games difficult.   **(1 mark)**
(b) .... likes finding music using technology.   **(1 mark)**
(c) .... likes the fact that some aspects of technology are not expensive.   **(1 mark)**
(d) .... thinks technology is not safe.   **(1 mark)**
(e) .... finds technology useful for schoolwork.   **(1 mark)**

15

The internet

There are lots of ways you can use the internet. This page will help you with this specific vocabulary.

Internet

Cuando estoy conectado/a a Internet suelo ...
When I am online I usually ...

hacer compras por Internet	do online shopping
navegar por la red	surf the net
cargar / subir fotos a Instagram	
upload photos to Instagram	
leer páginas web	read webpages
utilizar los chats	use chatrooms
enviar y recibir correos electrónicos	
send and receive emails	
buscar información	look for information
hacer ejercicios interactivos en línea	
do interactive online exercises	

Solía ver vídeos en YouTube.
I used to watch videos on YouTube.

Talking about what usually happens

You use the verb soler + the infinitive to talk about what someone **usually** does.

suelo	I usually ...
sueles	you usually (singular / informal) ...
suele	he / she usually ...
solemos	we usually ...
soléis	you usually (plural / informal) ...
suelen	they usually ...

Suelo descargar música.
I usually download music.

Knowing the **imperfect** form can help you improve your performance in listening tests.

Worked example

Traduce el texto siguiente **al español**.   (12 marks)

My friends and I use the internet nearly every day. At school we sometimes need to look for information or do online exercises in Spanish classes. Last week I made a webpage. Later I am going to upload photos of my party.

Mis amigos y yo utilizamos Internet casi todos los días. En el instituto a veces tenemos que buscar información o hacer ejercicios en línea durante las clases de español. La semana pasada hice una página web y fue bastante fácil. Más tarde voy a subir fotos de mi fiesta.

Aiming higher

For the translation task, be prepared to write sentences using verb forms that express present, past and sometimes future events. It is therefore really important to learn your verb endings carefully.

Remember that 'the internet' never uses an article and always takes a capital letter in Spanish: Utilizamos Internet casi todos los días.

Now try this

Traduce el texto siguiente **al español**. (12 marks)

Normally I do online shopping as it is cheap and quite easy. At home my parents usually send and receive emails but my sister and I read webpages and use chatrooms. Last year I bought a new mobile phone online. Today I am surfing the net to look for some headphones.

Pros and cons of technology

Use these phrases to prepare your own opinions on using technology.

La tecnología: las ventajas y los inconvenientes

permitir más comunicación e interacción
to allow more communication and interaction
hablar con la familia en el extranjero
to talk with family abroad
comprar y vender por Internet
to buy and sell online
jugar a videojuegos con amigos
to play videogames with friends
leer las noticias   **to read the news**

el peligro de   **the danger of**
conocer a extraños con malas intenciones
meeting strangers with bad intentions
ver contenido inapropiado y nocivo
watching inappropriate and harmful content
el acoso en las redes sociales
bullying on social networking sites
acceso a los datos personales
access to personal data

Using ser in different tenses

Recognising ser (to be) in the past, present and future is key for higher-level reading questions.

Present	Imperfect	Future
soy	era	seré
eres	eras	serás
es	era	será

El problema más grave será la piratería informática.
The most serious problem will be software piracy.

Escuchar y ver música por Internet es guay.
Listening to and watching music online is cool.

Worked example

Read this article about the internet.

> Existen muchos problemas con Internet. Antes, el problema más grave era el acoso en las redes sociales pero los expertos dicen que actualmente el problema más serio es el fraude en las cuentas bancarias. También dicen que dentro de diez años el contenido nocivo será el problema más grave.

Put a cross ✗ by the **one** correct sentence.   **(1 mark)**

☒ **A** There are lots of problems with the Internet.
☐ **B** Online bullying is the most serious problem.

- Knowing **ser** in the present, imperfect and future will enable you to distinguish between the problems.
- Time phrases – **antes** (before), **actualmente** (currently) and **dentro de diez años** (within ten years) – can also help distinguish time frames.

Now try this

What does the article in the worked example tell us? Put a cross ✗ in the **three** correct boxes.   **(3 marks)**

☐ **A** Social networking sites are always safe.
☐ **B** Fraud is now a bigger problem than online bullying.
☐ **C** Bank accounts are at risk from fraud.
☐ **D** In ten years, experts will solve the fraud issue.
☐ **E** Fraud will always be the main problem.
☐ **F** Websites with harmful content will become more of a problem.

Hobbies

Prepare to talk and write about hobbies using this page. Research any hobbies you do that aren't covered here so that you can talk about them easily.

El ocio

Juego con videojuegos.	I play video games.
Toco la batería.	I play the drums.
Hago piragüismo.	I do canoeing.
Voy en monopatín.	I skateboard.
Bailo.	I dance.
Voy / Salgo a caminar.	I go for walks.
Salgo con amigos.	I go out with friends.

Veo muchas series de televisión.

I watch lots of television series.

Mi pasatiempo preferido es el patinaje en línea.

My favourite hobby is rollerblading.

Escucha música.
She listens to music.

Present tense (regular verbs)

To form the present tense of regular verbs, replace the infinitive ending as follows:

Grammar page 88

	hablar – to speak	comer – to eat	vivir – to live
I	hablo	como	vivo
you	hablas	comes	vives
he / she / it	habla	come	vive
we	hablamos	comemos	vivimos
you	habláis	coméis	vivís
they	hablan	comen	viven

Some verbs have an irregular form in the present tense for the first person singular (yo).
hacer ➡ hago
salir ➡ salgo
ver ➡ veo
For more information on irregular verbs, go to page 90.

Worked example

 LISTENING TRACK 10

Listen and put a cross ✗ in the correct box.
(1 mark)

Javier likes …
☐ **A** listening to music   ☐ **C** going swimming
☒ **B** skateboarding   ☐ **D** watching TV

Listen to the recording

– ¿Qué te gusta hacer, Javier?
– Me encanta ir en monopatín. ¡Es fantástico!

Listening strategies

Learning vocabulary is key to completing listening tasks successfully. For each topic, make lists of words that you find difficult to remember and ask someone to test you on them.

Listen out for key nouns and verbs to help you answer. You cannot just rely on your knowledge of cognates. Here you need to know patinaje and natación as well as música and televisión.

Now try this

 LISTENING TRACK 11

Listen to the whole recording from the worked example and write Carmen, Teresa or Leonardo in the correct place. There are **three** correct answers.
(3 marks)

A loves reading ....
B goes shopping with friends ....
C likes the cinema ....
D goes swimming every day ....
E listens to modern music ....
F loves playing video games ....

Listen to the recording

Music

Make sure you are able to give your opinion about music and music events.

La música

Estoy aprendiendo a tocar …
I am learning to play …

el piano   la trompeta   el violín   la flauta dulce

la batería   la flauta   el saxofón   el clarinete

Fui a un concierto de música clásica.
I went to a classical music concert.
Escuché música rap.   I listened to rap music.
Fui al festival de música pop.
I went to the pop festival.
Tocaron muchas canciones famosas.
They played lots of famous songs.
Me encanta el rock.
I love rock music.

Describing events: preterite vs imperfect

To describe a music event, you use the **preterite** tense when you talk about **single/completed** events in the past.
Participamos en un espectáculo.
We took part in a show.
Anoche escuché a mi grupo favorito.
I listened to my favourite band last night.

Tocó la guitarra.
She played the guitar.

However, you use the **imperfect** tense when you describe **background** details.
Había un ambiente especial.
There was a special atmosphere.
El teatro era antiguo y grande.
The theatre was old and big.

Worked example

Answer the question as fully as possible.
• ¿Te gusta la música?

Sí, me gusta mucho y estoy aprendiendo a tocar el violín en la orquesta del instituto. Ayer un amigo mío y yo fuimos a un concierto de música clásica. Fue increíble.

Para mí, la música es muy importante, ya que nos puede dar mucho placer. Antes tocaba la flauta dulce pero ahora toco la trompeta. La música es importantísima en muchas celebraciones como bodas o fiestas de cumpleaños. El mes pasado fui a un espectáculo de música y baile tradicional en el pueblo donde vivo. El ambiente era tremendo y a todo el mundo le gustó escuchar tantas melodías fantásticas.

Using both present and past tenses – me gusta, fuimos – creates variety. Including a present continuous phrase – estoy aprendiendo a tocar – also helps to raise the language level.

Extending the response with further information (about why music is important) improves the content and uses more complex opinion language. This answer also employs a good range of tenses: present, preterite and imperfect. Using the superlative makes an ordinary adjective more interesting – importantísimo.

Now try this

Now you answer the same question.
• ¿Te gusta la música?

Try this yourself and then listen to the sample response to get some more ideas.

Listen to the recording

Sport

When you write about sport, remember to use the appropriate verb – jugar, practicar or hacer.

Los deportes

¿Qué deporte practicas?	What sport do you do?
Juego …	I play …

al fútbol.

al baloncesto.

al tenis.

Practico …   I do …

el ciclismo.

el jogging / footing.

la equitación.

la gimnasia.

Hago …   I do …

patinaje.

Using jugar and practicar

You use a different verb with different sports. Here are the three verbs in the main tenses.

	jugar	practicar	hacer
Present	juego	practico	hago
Preterite	jugué	practiqué	hice
Imperfect	jugaba	practicaba	hacía
Future	jugaré	practicaré	haré

Jugaba al squash, pero ahora no hago deporte. El año que viene haré vela.
I used to play squash but now I don't do any sport. Next year I'll do sailing.

Remember that jugar is followed by al with a masculine sport. Practico is followed by the article el or la, but there is no article after hago.

Worked example

Read this extract from the novel *Sara y las Goleadoras 1* by Laura Gallego, in which Sara is talking to Vicky.

– Ni hablar. No cuentes conmigo.
– Pero, Vicky … si a ti te gusta el deporte …
– Me gusta estar en forma, eso es todo. No sé jugar al fútbol.
– Pues aprendes.
– Pero me quitará tiempo para estudiar …
– Pues estudias menos.
– ¿¡Qué!? ¡Suspenderé!
– ¿Cómo vas a suspender? ¡Si tú siempre sacas buenas notas!
– Porque estudio.
– ¿Y no haces footing tres veces por semana? Pues peudes cambiarlo por los entrenamientos del equipo …
– ¡Pero si no hay equipo!
– Pues lo montamos.

Answer the following question **in English**.
What is Sara trying to persuade Vicky to do?   **(1 mark)**
Play football.

Reading literary texts strategies

✓ With some more challenging texts, you may have to make deductions that show you really understand the finer details of what you are reading.

✓ By spotting that the second speaker addresses Vicky, we know that she is Sara and that the first person to speak must be Vicky. When Vicky speaks again, she says that she likes being fit but doesn't know how to play football. So you can deduce that Sara must be trying to persuade her to play football.

Now try this

Read the extract again. Answer the following questions **in English**.

(a) Apart from Vicky's lack of experience, what other reason does she give for not getting involved?   **(1 mark)**

(b) Why is Vicky unlikely to follow Sara's suggestion about schoolwork?   **(1 mark)**

(c) What does Sara say about Vicky's school achievements?   **(1 mark)**

(d) What is Sara's final time-saving suggestion to Vicky?   **(1 mark)**

Reading

You should be able to give opinions on reading.

La lectura

Soy fanático/a de ...	I am fanatical about ...
Soy adicto/a a ...	I am addicted to ...
las revistas.	magazines.
los periódicos.	newspapers.
las novelas policíacas.	detective novels.
los libros electrónicos.	e-books.
Leo muchos libros.	I read lots of books.
Prefiero la ficción.	I prefer fiction.
Me ayuda a relajarme.	It helps me relax.
Me hace pensar.	It makes me think.
Es informativo.	It's informative.

Me gusta ir a las librerías.
I like to visit bookshops.

Expressing a range of opinions

Creo que ...	I think that ...
♥ Me gusta ...	I like ...
✗ No me gusta (nada) ...	I don't like ... (at all).
Odio ...	I hate ...
En mi opinión ...	In my opinion ...
Me interesa ...	I am interested in ...
Me chifla ...	I am really into ...

With verbs that are used in the third person (gustar, encantar, interesar, chiflar, etc.), remember to add –n if the subject is plural.

Me interesan los tebeos.
I'm interested in comics.
Me gustan los artículos sobre moda.
I like articles about fashion.

Worked example

Read the article about reading.

La lectura es una actividad tranquila que se puede hacer en casi cualquier lugar. No hay duda que expande significativamente la mente porque estimula la imaginación. A veces la lectura también nos ayuda a aprender nuevo vocabulario mientras uno se escapa de la realidad. Antes los jóvenes pasaban mucho más tiempo leyendo novelas o revistas pero ahora, con el dominio de la tecnología, el número de lectores adolescentes está disminuyendo.

Answer the question **in English**.
Where can you read? **(1 mark)**
almost anywhere

Think and make connections. Sometimes the answer to a seemingly straightforward question is a little more complex. Here the question suggests that the answer will be a particular location where you can read. However, the answer is more abstract: en casi cualquier lugar.

Use your knowledge of tenses to help you understand the final part of the text.

Now try this

Read the article from the worked example again and answer the questions **in English**.
(a) What positive effect does reading have? **(1 mark)**
(b) What can it sometimes help with? **(1 mark)**
(c) Summarise the changes mentioned in reading habits. **(1 mark)**

Films

Make sure you are able to talk about films and buy tickets at a cinema.

El cine

una comedia	a comedy
una película romántica	a romantic film
una película de dibujos animados	an animated film / cartoon
una película de ciencia ficción	a science-fiction film
una película de aventura	an adventure film
una película de suspense	a thriller
una película de terror / de miedo	a horror film
una película de artes marciales	a martial arts film

¿Quieres ir al cine el domingo?
Do you want to go to the cinema on Sunday?

No puedo, estoy ocupado/a.
I can't, I'm busy.

Me encantaría ir.   I would love to go.

Voy a sacar entradas por Internet.
I am going to buy tickets online.

¿Dónde nos encontramos?
Where shall we meet?

Podemos quedar en la estación.
We can meet at the station.

Days of the week

lunes	Monday
martes	Tuesday
miércoles	Wednesday
jueves	Thursday
viernes	Friday
sábado	Saturday
domingo	Sunday

To specify a day you regularly do something, use los:
Los sábados vemos películas.
On Saturdays we watch films.

To specify a particular day, use el:
Quedamos el lunes a las cinco de la tarde.
Let's meet on Monday at 5pm.

por la tarde / noche
in the afternoon / at night
los fines de semana   at weekends
todos los días   every day

Worked example

TRACK 13

Isabel is talking about films. Listen to the recording. Complete the sentence with the correct word from the box.

Listen to the recording

| week adventure fun martial arts |
| Saturday exciting interesting month |

Isabel prefers __adventure__ films.   **(1 mark)**

– Me chiflan las películas de artes marciales pero no son mis favoritas. En realidad, prefiero las películas de aventuras.

Exam alert

Make sure you **don't rush** to complete the task, or you could miss important details. Listen **carefully**, right to the end of the recording, before you make your final decision.

The key to choosing the correct answer is to identify which films she prefers rather than films she likes. She says **prefiero** for adventure films and uses **me chiflan** for martial arts films.

Now try this

TRACK 14

Listen to the recording

Listen to the whole recording from the worked example and complete the sentences with the correct word from the box.

(a) She likes adventure films because they are very .... **(1 mark)**

(b) Next .... she is going to watch a film at home. **(1 mark)**

TV

You need to be able to describe the **types** of programmes you watch, as well as naming them.

Los programas de televisión

los programas de deporte	sports programmes
el telediario / las noticias	news
los documentales	documentaries
los concursos	gameshows
las series de policías	police series
los dibujos animados	cartoons
las telenovelas	soaps
un programa de telerrealidad	a reality TV programme

Note that you always use the definite article (the) for the items you compare.

The comparative

Grammar page 85

The comparative is used to compare two things. It is formed as follows:

más + adjective + que = more ... than
menos + adjective + que = less ... than

The adjective agrees with the noun it describes:

Las telenovelas son menos aburridas que los concursos.
Soap operas are less boring than gameshows.

Los dibujos animados son más interesantes que los programas de telerrealidad.
Cartoons are more interesting than reality TV programmes.

Aiming higher

You need to give or understand **reasons** for your likes and dislikes. Use comparatives to impress!

Worked example

Read this advertisement for a television channel.

Canal Concurso es un canal nuevo que empezó en México hace tres meses. Ofrece una programación animada sin ser infantil. Se puede ver una gran variedad de concursos para todas las edades. Actualmente nuestro concurso más popular es de Japón, con subtítulos en español, y los participantes son niños de ocho a trece años. Hay que verlo. ¡Es sorprendente!

Answer the question **in English**.
How long has the channel been broadcasting? **(1 mark)**
3 months

Aiming higher

Look at **Spanish websites** about films and TV programmes. Not only will you practise your vocabulary, you'll also develop good reading strategies that will help you in the exam, such as:
- ✓ using what you know to rule out some options
- ✓ recognising cognates
- ✓ using grammar structures to help work out unknown words.

Now try this

Read the text from the worked example again and answer the questions **in English**.

(a) How does the advertisement describe the programmes the channel shows? **(1 mark)**
(b) Who are the gameshows on the channel for? **(1 mark)**
(c) Where is the most popular show from? **(1 mark)**
(d) Who can go on this show? **(1 mark)**

Celebrations

Be prepared to talk about how you and your family celebrate.

¡Felicidades!

la fiesta de cumpleaños	birthday party
la boda	wedding
el aniversario	anniversary
la Nochebuena	Christmas Eve
la Nochevieja	New Year's Eve
Papá Noel	Father Christmas
el Día de Reyes	Epiphany (6th January)
la Semana Santa	Easter

¡Feliz Navidad!
Happy Christmas

¡Felices Pascuas!
Happy Easter

¡Feliz cumpleaños!
Happy birthday

¡Feliz Año Nuevo!
Happy New Year

Using different tenses

Present

Normalmente, celebramos ...
Normally, we celebrate ...
Vienen nuestros abuelos / primos.
Our grandparents / cousins come.

Preterite

Invité a ...	I invited ...
Comimos ...	We ate ...
¡Fue (genial)!	It was (great)!

Imperfect

Antes íbamos a ...	We used to go to ...
Había mucha gente.	There were a lot of people.

Future

Iremos a ...	We will go to ...
Será (fantástico).	It will be (fantastic).

Worked example

Escribe un blog sobre las celebraciones.   (20 marks)

> Normalmente, para celebrar mi cumpleaños voy al cine. Cumplí quince años el fin de semana pasado. Por la tarde fui al cine con mis mejores amigos y por la noche celebramos una fiesta en casa. Invité a diez amigos y mis primos vinieron también. Lo pasé fenomenal.

Here the preterite tense has been used successfully (cumplí, fui, invité, vinieron, etc.). The student has also included an opinion (lo pasé fenomenal).

Aiming Higher

> Siempre celebramos mi cumpleaños, la Semana Santa, la Navidad y la Nochevieja en casa con toda la familia. La Navidad me parece el día más emocionante del año porque siempre lo celebramos con mucha comida, y varios regalos. Hace dos años estuvimos en España y me encantó ver cómo se celebra el Día de Reyes pero este año nos quedaremos en casa.

This has a greater variety of vocabulary and present, preterite and future tenses (celebramos, estuvimos, nos quedaremos). Interesting and complex structures also raise the level of the description (la Navidad me parece ... , me encantó ver cómo se celebra ...).

Now try this

Escribe un blog sobre tus celebraciones en casa. **Debes** incluir los puntos siguientes:
- lo que haces normalmente para tu cumpleaños
- lo que hiciste la Navidad pasada
- por qué son importantes las celebraciones
- los planes para una celebración en el futuro.

Escribe aproximadamente 80–90 palabras **en español**.   (20 marks)

Festivals

Learn vocabulary on this topic so you can understand descriptions of festivals in Spain.

Fiestas

España es famosa por sus fiestas.
Spain is famous for its festivals.
Algunas son de naturaleza religiosa y
  otras son históricas.
Some are religious in character and
  others are historical.
Muchas se celebran cada año.
Many are celebrated every year.
Tienen lugar en …   They take place in …
  el aire libre.   the open air.
  el centro urbano.   the city centre.
  las aldeas.   the small villages.
Las calles están cerradas al tráfico.
The streets are closed to traffic.
Es una tradición popular.
It's a popular tradition.
Hay fuegos artificiales. There are fireworks.
Mucha gente participa en desfiles.
A lot of people take part in processions.
Se visten con trajes tradicionales.
People are dressed in traditional clothes.
Mucha gente baila.   Lots of people dance.

Using se to avoid the passive

The passive voice ('is celebrated', 'was celebrated', etc.) is used frequently in English but is often avoided in Spanish by using the reflexive pronoun se.
La fiesta se celebra una vez al año.
The festival is celebrated once a year.
This translates literally as: The festival celebrates itself once a year.
The reflexive pronoun agrees with the subject.
Se llevan trajes de flamenco.
Flamenco costumes are worn.
Se lanzan tomates.   Tomatoes are thrown.
El pueblo se convierte en …
The village becomes …
La famosa Feria de Abril se celebra en Sevilla.
The famous April fair is celebrated in Seville.
El pueblo se llena de música y ruido.
The town is filled with music and noise.

Worked example

Mira la foto y prepara tus respuestas a los puntos siguientes:

- la descripción de la foto
- tu opinión sobre la importancia de las fiestas
- tu experiencia de una fiesta reciente
- !

En esta foto se ve una fiesta tradicional con muchos fuegos artificiales magníficos. En la foto hay mucha gente y parece un espectáculo fantástico. A mí me encantaría ir a esta fiesta. … Para mí las fiestas son muy importantes porque nos dan la oportunidad de entender más de la cultura de un lugar y de formar parte de un grupo grande de gente de varias edades. Además son muy divertidas. … El año pasado mi familia y yo fuimos a una fiesta tradicional del pueblo pequeño donde vivo. Se cerraron las calles al tráfico y bailamos mucho. …

Exam alert

When you talk about a photo for the second task in your speaking exam, you will be asked to talk about each bullet in order. In this task the examiner would ask these questions in this order:

– Describe la foto.
– Creo que las fiestas no tienen mucho valor. ¿Qué opinas tú?
– Háblame de tu experiencia de una fiesta reciente.
– [an unexpected question]

The whole task should last three and a half minutes, so for each bullet you should try to speak for at least 45 seconds.

Now try this

Talk about the photo in the worked example. Include information for each of the bullet points. Also answer this question:

- ¿Hay alguna fiesta española a la que te gustaría ir?

Try to talk for at least three and a half minutes.

Holiday preferences

This page will help you express your opinions on holidays in lots of different ways.

Prefiero las vacaciones …

🙂	🙁
Prefiero las vacaciones en la playa con amigos. I prefer holidays on the beach with friends.	No me gusta ir de vacaciones con mis padres. I don't like going on holiday with my parents.
Mis vacaciones ideales serían en el Caribe. My ideal holiday would be in the Caribbean.	No soporto hacer camping. I can't stand going camping.
Es maravilloso conocer una ciudad y perderme por las calles estrechas. It's wonderful getting to know a city and losing myself in the narrow streets.	Odio los sitios arruinados por el turismo descontrolado. I hate places ruined by uncontrolled tourism.
Siempre he querido visitar Australia. I have always wanted to visit Australia.	El hotel donde nos quedamos no admite perros. The hotel where we are staying doesn't allow dogs.
Es relajante descansar sin pensar en el instituto. It's relaxing to take it easy without thinking about school.	Odio el sol porque siempre me pongo rojo. I hate the sun as it always makes me red.
	Me aburren los museos y la historia. Museums and history bore me.

Worked example

Describe tus vacaciones ideales.   (20 marks)

> Mis vacaciones ideales serían en España. Diría que las vacaciones en España sin padres son fenomenales pero ellos lo pagan todo, así que con padres no están tan mal.

This question allows use of the **conditional** to say what your favourite type of holiday would be.

This answer includes a variety of tenses and complex phrases (me parece muy bonito). It also expresses different opinions.

Aiming Higher

> Mis vacaciones ideales serían en India. Podría visitar ciudades famosas como Mumbai and Jaipur. Me apasionan el arte y la arquitectura. Además, la comida es excelente. En Jaipur, visitaría el palacio de Hawa Mahal, que es un edificio magnífico construido en piedra rosa. El nombre significa Palacio de los Vientos, que me parece muy bonito. ¡Seguramente viajaré a India algún día!

Aiming higher

Try to include **more complex** language.

Mis padres siempre quieren que vaya con ellos.
My parents always want me to go with them.

Si pudiera, iría a Ibiza para ir de fiesta.
If I could, I'd go to Ibiza to party.

Now try this

Escribe un artículo sobre las vacaciones perfectas. **Debes** incluir los puntos siguientes:

- adónde prefieres ir de vacaciones
- lo que no te gusta hacer en las vacaciones
- lo que hiciste el año pasado
- adónde irás el año que viene y por qué.

Escribe aproximadamente 80–90 palabras **en español**.

(20 marks)

Hotels

Be prepared to take part in conversations about booking accommodation.

En un hotel

Quiero reservar …

una habitación individual / doble.

sin baño.

con ducha / balcón.

para siete noches

¿A qué hora sirven el desayuno / la cena?

con vistas al mar / a la piscina / a la montaña

la recepción

la llave

el ascensor

media pensión

pensión completa

conexión a Internet

quince días

I'd like to reserve …

a single / double room.

without a bathroom.

with a shower / balcony.

for seven nights

What time is breakfast / dinner served?

with a sea / pool / mountain view

reception

key

lift

half board

full board

internet connection

fortnight

Revising numbers

Grammar page 105

Here are a few ideas:

✓ **Look at** the numbers on page 105.
Can you identify any patterns that will help you remember them?
– 16 to 19 are dieci + 6, dieci + 7, etc.
– 31, 41, 51, etc. are always y uno (but 21 is different)
– tres / trece / treinta

✓ **Practise** numbers on your own: count in twos, in threes, in fives. Count backwards! Or practise playing bingo with a friend!

Worked example

You are in a hotel in Spain. The teacher will play the part of the receptionist and speak first.

Usted está en un hotel en España. Está hablando con el/la recepcionista. Quiere reservar una habitación.

1. Habitación – tipo

¿En qué puedo servirle?

Quiero una habitación doble con ducha, por favor.

2. Noches – número

Muy bien. ¿Para cuántas noches?

Me gustaría la habitación para cinco noches.

3. !

¿Prefiere una habitación con vistas al mar o a la montaña?

Prefiero una habitación con vistas al mar.

4. Planes – mañana

De acuerdo. ¿Tiene planes para mañana?

Sí, vamos a visitar el castillo y luego nos gustaría ir a un restaurante típico.

5. ? Desayuno – precio

¿Tiene una pregunta?

¿El desayuno está incluido en el precio de la habitación?

Sí, está incluido.

Exam alert

Role play strategies
This topic lends itself very well to a role play. Use the preparation time for the speaking exam to read the role play prompts carefully and to decide what you will say for each one. Remember that you can reuse the vocabulary from the prompt. For example:

Habitación – tipo ➡

Quiero una habitación doble. (I would like a double room.)

Now try this

Listen to the recording

Prepare your own answers to these role play prompts.
Listen to the recording of the teacher parts and fill in your parts in the pauses.

1. Habitación – tipo
2. Noches – número
3. !
4. Planes – mañana
5. ? Desayuno – precio

Camping

Learn the vocabulary here to help you understand texts about campsites.

El camping

¡Vamos a acampar!	Let's camp!
el camping	the campsite
Está en el campo.	It's in the countryside.
una tienda	a tent
una caravana	a caravan
un cubo para basura	a rubbish bin
una piscina cubierta	an indoor pool
una lavandería automática	a launderette
una tienda de comestibles	a grocery shop
una sala de juegos	a games room
un cajero automático	a cash machine
las duchas	the showers
la ropa de cama	bed linen
un saco de dormir	a sleeping bag
el alquiler de bicicletas	bike hire

Es obligatorio apagar las luces a medianoche.
It is compulsory to turn off lights at midnight.

No se permite hacer ruido.
Being noisy is not allowed.

No se permiten animales.
Animals are not allowed.

Using different verbs

To make your writing and speaking more varied, don't just use different tenses – use different verbs too. Make lists in diagrams like this:

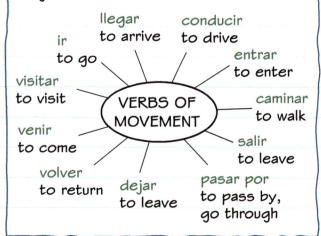

ir to go, llegar to arrive, conducir to drive, entrar to enter, caminar to walk, salir to leave, pasar por to pass by, go through, dejar to leave, volver to return, venir to come, visitar to visit — VERBS OF MOVEMENT

Note: Use se permite if it refers to a single thing, but se permiten if it refers to more than one thing.

Worked example

Read the texts.

En el camping
- El horario de silencio es de 01.00 a 07.00. Durante estas horas, se prohíbe la circulación de vehículos.
- No se permite hacer carreras de bicicletas.
- Están prohibidos los juegos de pelota cerca de las tiendas.
- El volumen o sonido de los aparatos de televisión debe ser, durante todo el día, lo más bajo posible.

En el albergue juvenil
- No se permite hacer ruido después de medianoche.
- No se permite comer en los dormitorios.
- Es obligatorio traer el saco de dormir.
- Es obligatorio utilizar los cubos para basura.

Reading strategies

Students perform well in tasks like this when they have a good knowledge of basic vocabulary items and use deductive reasoning. Use your ability to think, as well as your knowledge of Spanish!

Put a cross ✗ in the correct box. **(1 mark)**
In the campsite you are allowed to …
- ☐ **A** play ball games throughout the site
- ☒ **B** drive your car at 8am
- ☐ **C** have your TV on at any volume during the day
- ☐ **D** race bicycles

To answer this question correctly, you need to use the context of the texts and take advantage of the cognates to deduce that circulación de vehículos means 'driving vehicles'.

Now try this

Now read the texts from the worked example again and answer the questions **in English**.

(a) Where should you stay if you like to listen to music after midnight? **(1 mark)**

(b) Where do you need your own sleeping bag? **(1 mark)**

Accommodation

This page will help you to say more about holidays and to express your opinions.

El alojamiento

Estoy en …	I am staying in …
Me alojo en …	I stay in …
un camping	a campsite
un hotel de tres estrellas	a three-star hotel
un albergue juvenil	a youth hostel
una pensión / un hostal	a guest house
nuestro apartamento de Francia	our flat in France
alquilar	to hire, rent
una caravana	a caravan
un piso alquilado	a rented flat
una casa	a house
Prefiero quedarme en un hotel.	I prefer staying in a hotel.

Using me gusta(n) and me encanta(n)

Grammar page 101

Me gusta (I like) literally translates as 'it pleases me'. The thing that does the pleasing (i.e. the thing I like) is the subject. If this subject is plural, use me gustan.

Me encanta behaves in the same way.

Me gusta dormir al aire libre.
I like sleeping outdoors.

Me encanta alquilar un apartamento.
I love renting a flat.

And to say what you don't like …

No me gusta quedarme en un camping.
I don't like staying on a campsite.

Aiming higher

Using quedarse as well as alojarse in the **preterite** and **future** will show off your knowledge of the language.

me quedé / me alojé	I stayed
me quedaré / me alojaré	I will stay

me gusta ♥
me gusta mucho ♥ ♥
me encanta ♥ ♥ ♥

Worked example

Mira la foto y prepara las respuestas a los siguientes puntos:
- la descripción de la foto
- tu opinión de las vacaciones en un camping
- la última vez que fuiste de vacaciones
- !

En esta foto se ve una familia que está de vacaciones en un camping con su caravana. … Normalmente voy a un camping bastante aburrido pero el año pasado me quedé en un hotel precioso de cinco estrellas. … El año que viene voy a ir a un parador de lujo. Prefiero quedarme en un hotel porque no me gusta dormir al aire libre. … Me encantan los hoteles lujosos.

Speaking strategies

In the picture-based tasks, you will be asked a question for each of the bullet points. Remember that as part of this task you will also have to answer an unexpected question (!). Use the preparation time to make notes on key verbs and tenses that you will use for each bullet point.

Now try this

Talk about the photo in the worked example. Include information for each of the bullet points. Also talk about:
- tus vacaciones ideales

Try to talk for at least three minutes.

You will need the conditional to describe your ideal holidays. Rather than just saying me gustaría, try to vary the verbs you use: iría a … , me alojaría en … .

Holiday destinations

Make sure you know the future tense in order to talk about where you will go on holiday.

Adónde ir de vacaciones

Iré ...	I will go ...
a la costa.	to the coast.
a la montaña.	to the mountains.
a la playa.	to the beach.
al campo.	to the countryside.
a lugares culturales.	to cultural sites.
Descansaré.	I will rest.
Nadaré.	I will swim.
Haré yoga.	I will do yoga.
Iré a clases de baile.	I will go to dance classes.
Haré una excursión en bicicleta.	I will go on a cycling tour.
Veré lugares de interés.	I will see places of interest.
Montaré a caballo.	I will go horseriding.
Patinaré.	I will skate.
Esquiaré.	I will ski.
Haré alpinismo.	I will go rock climbing.
Haré vela.	I will go sailing.

The future tense

Grammar page 95

To form the future tense of most verbs, add the following endings to the infinitive:

	ir – to go
I will go	iré
you will go	irás
he / she / it will go	irá
we will go	iremos
you will go	iréis
they will go	irán

¿Adónde irás de vacaciones el año que viene?

Where will you go on holiday next year?

Iré a Grecia y haré una excursión en bicicleta.

I'll go to Greece and I'll go on a cycling tour.

Worked example

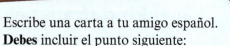

Escribe una carta a tu amigo español.
Debes incluir el punto siguiente:

• los planes para tus próximas vacaciones.

> Esquiaré en Francia con mi instituto. Va a ser genial. Nos quedaremos en un hotel cerca de la montaña.

> El año que viene iré a la costa de Italia con mi novio. Creo que va a ser perfecto porque serán nuestras primeras vacaciones juntos. Descansaremos en la playa y mi novio dará una vuelta en bicicleta. A mi me encantan los caballos, así que montaré en caballo cada día.

Using the **future** and the **near future** shows variety of tense usage. Adding more **detail** (where you will stay) can improve the content.

• Extending opinions by justifying them using connectives (**y, porque**) will help you if you are aiming higher.
• You can also use interesting phrases to show your grasp of a wider range of vocabulary, e.g. **nuestras primeras vacaciones juntos** (our first holiday together).

Now try this

Write your own response to the bullet point in the worked example about your holiday plans for next year. Write about 30–40 words.

Travelling

As well as revising ticket vocabulary, make sure you know your numbers for times and prices.

Comprar billetes

Quiero dos billetes para…	I would like two tickets to …
un billete de ida	a single ticket
un billete de ida y vuelta	a return ticket
para hoy / mañana	for today / tomorrow
¿A qué hora sale / llega?	What time does it depart / arrive?
Es directo.	It's direct.
un bonobús	a ticket for ten bus trips
¿Cuánto cuesta?	How much does it cost?
¿Hay descuento para los jóvenes?	Is there a discount for young people?
¿Cuánto tiempo dura el viaje?	How long does the journey take?
Dura …	It takes …
el próximo / último tren	the next / last train
Acaba de llegar / salir.	It has just arrived / departed.

Using para and por for 'for'

Grammar page 102

Use these rules to work out whether to use para or por.

Por – cause
Gracias por su ayuda. Thanks for your help.
Por – expressing rates
Vuelos a Madrid por 50 euros. Flights to Madrid for 50 euros.
Para – purpose
Quiero un billete de ida para el sábado. I want a single ticket for Saturday.
Para – a destination
Salió para Granada. He left for Granada.
Para – period of time in the future
Quiero una habitación para una semana. I would like a room for a week.

Worked example

LISTENING TRACK 16

Listen to the conversation at the train station and put a cross ✗ in the correct box. **(1 mark)**

The man wants …

- ✗ **A** a single ticket
- ☐ **B** a return ticket
- ☐ **C** a ticket to Valencia
- ☐ **D** a ticket for tomorrow

Listen to the recording

– Quiero un billete de ida para Sevilla para hoy.

Listening strategies

Students often find multiple-choice questions tricky, as it's easy to be put off by the wrong answers.

- ✓ Look at the options carefully before you listen.
- ✓ Try to predict what you are going to hear.
- ✓ Revise numbers and times, as they crop up in many contexts!

Now try this

LISTENING TRACK 17

Listen to the recording

Listen to the conversations from the worked example and put a cross ✗ in the correct box for each question.

	A	B	C	D	
1. The man's train will leave at …	☐ 14.50	☐ 15.50	☐ 15.40	☐ 16.50	**(1 mark)**
2. The woman buys a ticket for …	☐ today	☐ tomorrow	☐ next week	☐ Friday	**(1 mark)**
3. The woman's ticket costs …	☐ 13 euros	☐ 67 euros	☐ 79 euros	☐ 176 euros	**(1 mark)**

Holiday activities

Be prepared to talk about a wide range of activities that you enjoy doing on holiday.

Las actividades de vacaciones

¿Qué haces normalmente cuando estás de vacaciones?

What do you normally do on holiday?

Voy con mi familia / mis amigos a la playa.

I go with my family / friends to the beach.

Descanso / me relajo.	I relax.
Hago fotos.	I take photos.
Pinto y dibujo.	I paint and I draw.

Me baño en el mar.

Voy a discotecas.

Hago surfing.

Hago piragüismo.

Monto en bici.

Hago excursiones.

Hago esquí.

Worked example

SPEAKING

- ¿Qué haces normalmente cuando estás de vacaciones?

  Voy a Portugal con mis amigos. Es divertido porque vamos a discotecas. Nunca voy con mis padres porque es un rollo.

Aiming Higher

  Siempre voy de vacaciones con mi hermana. Tiene dos años más que yo, por lo que tenemos los mismos gustos. El año pasado fuimos a Ibiza. ¡Fue estupendo! Nos bañamos en el mar y descansamos en la playa. Por las noches íbamos a las discotecas y bailábamos hasta las tres de la mañana. Yo creo que a mis padres les gustaría que fuéramos con ellos pero sería aburrido.

Now try this

SPEAKING

Answer this question. Talk for about one minute.

- ¿Qué haces normalmente cuando estás de vacaciones?

Review the **present tense** (see page 88) to prepare yourself for this topic. Don't just revise 'I' forms – be ready to talk about what your friends and family do on holiday too, and what you do together.

Holiday experiences

Make sure you know how to use the preterite tense, so you can talk about your experiences.

Vacaciones pasadas

¿Adónde fuiste de vacaciones el año pasado?
Where did you go on holiday last year?

el verano pasado	last summer
hace dos años	two years ago
Fui con mi familia / con mis amigos / solo/a.	I went with my family / with my friends / alone.
Me alojé / Me quedé …	I stayed …
Viajé en …	I travelled by …
Hice un intercambio.	I did an exchange.
Pasé una semana allí.	I spent one week there.
Hice un viaje con el instituto.	I went on a school trip.

Preterite tense

Grammar page 93

These verbs in the preterite will be useful for talking about past holidays.

	visitar – to visit	comer – to eat	salir – to go out
I	visité	comí	salí
you	visitaste	comiste	saliste
he/she/it	visitó	comió	salió
we	visitamos	comimos	salimos
you	visitasteis	comisteis	salisteis
they	visitaron	comieron	salieron

Useful verbs in the preterite for talking about holidays include:

vi	I saw
bebí	I drank
hice	I did
fue	it was
tuve	I had

Bebí un zumo de naranja.

Worked example

Read this extract from the novel *Donde aprenden a volar las gaviotas* by Ana Alcolea where Arturo is talking about his summer holidays spent in Norway.

Dos días después de mi llegada, aquella ciudad me parecía aburrida: a las cinco de la tarde ya estaba todo cerrado y no había casi nadie por las calles de nuestro barrio. Cada trayecto de autobús costaba veinticinco coronas, o sea, tres euros, y pedalear hasta el centro en bicicleta no tenía ninguna gracia, así que lo estaba pasando fatal. El padre de Erik, el superprofesor, me miraba como si fuera un bicho raro: no concebía que a mis quince años todavía no fuera capaz de seguir una conversación en inglés. Me metía en mi habitación, intentaba estudiar y aprender frases para luego emplearlas con la familia.

Answer the following question **in English**.
When did Arturo start to find the town boring? **(1 mark)**
Two days after his arrival

Reading literary texts strategies

✓ If you find literary passages difficult, don't be put off so that you give up. There may be difficult sections in it but you may not need to understand these sections to answer the questions. The questions will only target parts of the extract where the vocabulary is what you can reasonably be expected to cope with.

The Spanish word for 'boring' is very well known – **aburrido** – so skim read until you find the word in the text. Then try to read around the word. The answer is likely to be in the words just before or just after the key item of vocabulary 'boring'. In this case, the beginning of the sentence, before **aburrido**, gives us the answer: **dos días después de mi llegada** – two days after my arrival.

Now try this

Read the extract again. Answer the following questions **in English**.

(a) What was the town like at five o'clock in the afternoon? **(2 marks)**

(b) How could Arturo have got into the town centre? **(2 marks)**

(c) What was Arturo constantly making an effort to do? **(2 marks)**

(d) How old was Arturo at the time? **(1 mark)**

Transport and directions

Use this vocabulary to talk about transport and understand or give directions.

El transporte

¿Vas a pie o en coche?
Do you walk or go by car?

Normalmente voy ... | Normally I travel ...
en coche. | by car.
en metro. | by underground.
en tren. | by train.
en barco. | by boat.
en moto. | by motorbike.
en ciclomotor. | by moped.
en autocar. | by coach.
en avión. | by plane.
la parada de autobús | bus stop
la vía para bicicletas | cycle path
el alquiler de coches | car hire
la zona peatonal | pedestrian zone
la conexión / el enlace | connection

El viaje dura una hora.
The journey takes an hour.

El metro está muy cerca.
The underground station is very close.

Prefiero coger el autobús.
I prefer to catch the bus.

Odio andar / ir a pie.   I hate walking.

Me gusta viajar en avión pero es caro.
I like to travel by plane but it is expensive.

Giving directions

You will need to understand and give directions.

Dobla a la derecha. | Dobla a la izquierda. | Sigue todo recto.

Toma la primera calle a la izquierda. | Toma la segunda calle a la derecha. | Toma la tercera calle a la derecha.

Cruza el puente. | Pasa el semáforo.

- Note cojo – I catch.
- el for all transport except la bicicleta / la moto.
- en coche (by car), etc. but a pie (on foot).

Worked example

Listen to the conversation with Lucía and answer the following question **in English**.
How does Lucía prefer to go to school?   **(1 mark)**
walking

Listen to the recording

– Hola Lucía, ¿cómo vas al instituto?
– Generalmente voy en coche, pero prefiero ir andando.

Exam alert

Remember that you do not need to answer in full sentences.

Make sure that you can recognise verbs in different forms, such as the gerund, e.g. andando (walking).

Now try this

Now listen to the whole conversation from the worked example and answer the following questions **in English**.

Listen to the recording

(a) Why does she prefer to walk to school?   **(1 mark)**
(b) What does she sometimes do?   **(1 mark)**

Transport problems

You will need to deal with problems linked to travelling and transport.

Problemas de transporte

Hay grandes retrasos.	There are long delays.
Los semáforos no funcionan.	
The traffic lights are not working.	
Los atascos son peores que el año pasado.	
The traffic jams are worse than last year.	
Hay demasiados camiones.	There are too many lorries.
Hemos perdido el vuelo.	We have missed the flight.
El aparcamiento está lleno.	The car park is full.
Mi coche no tiene gasolina.	My car has no petrol.
¿Qué pasó?	What happened?
Tuvieron un accidente ...	They had an accident ...
en la autopista.	on the motorway.
en la carretera.	on the road.
en la calle.	in the street.
Hubo una colisión entre diez vehículos.	
There was a crash involving ten vehicles.	
Un peatón cruzó la calle sin mirar.	
A pedestrian crossed the street without looking.	
No ha habido / hubo heridos.	No one was injured.

How to say 'because of'

In Spanish, there are several ways to describe what has caused an event or situation:

☑ a causa de   because of
A causa de una huelga en Francia, no hay vuelos a Paris.
Because of a strike in France there are no flights to Paris.

☑ debido a   due to
Debido a una tormenta en Nueva York, el vuelo IB6789 va con retraso.
Due to a storm in New York flight IB6789 is delayed.

☑ gracias a   thanks to
Gracias a Iberia, llegaré a tiempo.
Thanks to Iberia, I will arrive on time.

El conductor no vio al ciclista.
The driver did not see the cyclist.

Worked example

Read the texts about recent accidents.

Complete the following sentence.
Enter either **Cristina**, **Alejandro**, **Miguel** or **Isabel**.

..Miguel.. was delayed by two hours.

(1 mark)

Cristina: Fue horrible. Hubo una colisión entre un camión grande y dos peatones en la calle cerca de mi casa.

Alejandro: Ayer vi un accidente en la carretera. No hubo heridos pero había un retraso de veinte minutos debido a eso.

Miguel: En la autopista hubo un accidente muy grave entre dos coches. Llevaron a los conductores al hospital, y después de marcharse la ambulancia, estuvimos dos horas en un atasco enorme.

Isabel: Siempre hay muchos accidentes en la carretera principal cerca de mi instituto a causa de los coches que van demasiado rápido.

Now try this

Read the text in the worked example again. Complete the following sentences. Enter either **Cristina**, **Alejandro**, **Miguel** or **Isabel**. You can use each person more than once.

(a) .... saw an accident but no one was hurt.   **(1 mark)**

(b) .... describes an accident involving a lorry.   **(1 mark)**

(c) .... thinks people drive too fast.   **(1 mark)**

(d) .... writes about a motorway crash.   **(1 mark)**

(e) .... mentions that pedestrians were involved in an accident.   **(1 mark)**

When choosing the correct person for a reading task, you must read **all** of the texts before you begin to look for **specific details** mentioned in the statements.

Holiday problems

Lots of things can go wrong on holiday! Make sure you know how to say them in Spanish.

En el hotel

Quiero quejarme. — I want to complain.

La luz no funciona. — The light does not work.

El aire acondicionado no funciona.
The air conditioning does not work.

No hay calefacción. — There is no heating.

No hay toallas. — There are no towels.

Necesito dos almohadas. — I need two pillows.

La habitación no está limpia.
The room is not clean.

Me hace falta papel higiénico / jabón.
I need toilet paper / soap.

El baño / El aseo está sucio.
The bathroom / toilet is dirty.

Falta una cucharita. — There's a teaspoon missing.

No está bien hecho. — It is not cooked properly.

¿Me puede traer unas servilletas?
Please can you bring me some napkins?

No hay ni aceite ni vinagre.
There is no oil or vinegar.

La comida está demasiado salada.
The food is too salty.

Using the verb faltar

Some Spanish verbs are only used in the **third person** singular and plural. Faltar is the verb to use if something is missing or needed. You use the plural form when you need more than one thing.

Falta una cuchara.
There's a spoon missing.

Faltan un cuchillo y un tenedor.
There's a knife and fork missing.

You can use hacer falta in the same way.

Me hace falta un plato.
I need a plate.

Me hacen falta sábanas limpias.
I need some clean sheets.

Quiero un reembolso. –
I would like a refund.
Quiero cambiar de habitación. –
I would like to change rooms.

Worked example

Read the text about restaurants. Put a cross ✗ in the correct box.

(1 mark)

● ● ●

Los problemas de servicio al cliente

¡Comida fría!
Hay muchos problemas que uno se puede encontrar en un restaurante, pero lo que realmente puede llegar a irritar a un cliente es cuando la comida llega fría. Es una señal clara de que el camarero no está haciendo bien su trabajo.

¡Camareros perdidos!
Otro problema que puede hacer que la experiencia en un restaurante no sea tan buena, es cuando necesitas al camarero y no le puedes encontrar por ninguna parte. Quieres pedir la comida o más bebidas y nunca está cerca de tu mesa. Los buenos camareros siempre están pendientes de sus clientes y de lo que necesitan.

¡Platos sucios!
Platos, cuchillos, tenedores y en definitiva, un restaurante sucio, es terrible siempre. Los camareros deberían limpiar las mesas con regularidad y asegurarse de que todo lo que pongan en la mesa esté bien limpio. ¡Nadie quiere encontrarse con una mosca en la sopa!

Clients become annoyed when …
- ☐ **A** the waiter is rude or unfriendly
- ☐ **B** the waiter keeps coming back to the table
- ☒ **C** their meal is not hot
- ☐ **D** they are not given the bill quickly

Exam alert

Multiple choice questions with four options (A, B, C, D) are used in both listening and reading papers. Make sure you follow the instructions and put a **cross** in **one box only**. If you make a mistake, draw a line through it and then put a clear cross in another box.

Now try this

Read the text again in the worked example and answer these questions **in English**.

(a) What does food arriving cold at the table tell the customer? **(1 mark)**

(b) What should waiters do regularly? **(1 mark)**

Asking for help abroad

You need to be able to ask for help if you run into trouble while abroad.

En el extranjero

Necesito ayuda.   I need help.

El coche ha tenido una avería.
The car has broken down.

Quiero denunciar el robo de ...
I want to report the theft of ...

El ladrón era bajo y llevaba gafas.
The thief was short and wore glasses.

No sufrí ningún daño personal.
I did not suffer any physical injury.

Tomó lugar en la estación de servicio.
It took place in the petrol station.

¿Puede darme una ficha oficial?
Can you give me an official form?

No sé dónde está el billetero.
I don't know where my wallet is.

En la oficina de objetos perdidos

He perdido ...	I have lost ...
un anillo	a ring
un bolso	a bag
un collar	a necklace
unas gafas de sol	some sunglasses
unas llaves	some keys
un ordenador portátil	a laptop
un paraguas	an umbrella
unos pendientes	some earrings
una pulsera	a bracelet
un sombrero	a hat

Worked example

You have lost something and are in a lost property office in Valencia.
The teacher will play the role of the lost property officer and will speak first.

Usted está en la oficina de objetos perdidos de Valencia (España).
Usted ha perdido algo.

1. Objeto – descripción
   ¿En qué puedo servirle?
   He perdido mi paraguas.
   Es azul y pequeño.

2. En Valencia – motivo
   ¿Qué hace aquí en España?
   Estoy de vacaciones en
   Valencia con mi familia.

3. !
   ¿Dónde y cuándo lo ha perdido?
   Lo perdí ayer en el museo.
   Lo siento, pero aquí no está.

4. ? Volver (día) – oficina
   ¿Tiene una pregunta?
   ¿Cuándo puedo volver otra vez?
   A lo mejor el lunes.

5. ? Horario – oficina
   ¿Tiene otra pregunta?
   ¿Cuál es el horario de
   la oficina?
   Abrimos a las diez y cerramos
   a las siete y media.

Exam alert

This is a Higher tier role play:
it has five prompts and one
unprepared question, and you
have to ask two questions.
You are expected to use
different tenses in your answers.

Revise question words to
help you create questions for
the role play task.
¿Qué? – What?
¿Cómo? – How? What?
¿Dónde? – Where?
¿Cuándo? – When?
¿A qué hora? – At what time?
¿Con quién? – With whom?

Now try this

Listen to the recording

Use the vocabulary on
this page to help you
create your answers.

Imagine you have had your purse stolen in a café. How would you answer these role play questions?
Prepare your answers, then listen to the recording and fill in the pauses with your answers.

1. ¿Qué ha ocurrido exactamente?
2. ¿Dónde ha tenido lugar el robo?
3. ¿Puede describir al ladrón / a la ladrona?
4. ¿Cómo es su monedero?

Eating in a café

Make sure you revise lots of café vocabulary for understanding texts and role play situations.

Comer en la cafetería

¿Qué va a tomar?	What would you like?
Voy a tomar …	I'll have …
agua con gas.	sparkling mineral water.
un café (solo).	a (black) coffee.
una limonada.	a lemonade.
un té.	a tea.
un zumo de naranja.	an orange juice.
con azúcar	with sugar
con leche	with milk
con / sin hielo	with / without ice
un bocadillo	a sandwich
una hamburguesa	a hamburger
un helado	an ice cream
un perrito caliente	a hot dog
un vaso	a glass
una botella	a bottle
una taza	a cup

High-frequency words

Watch out for key but easily overlooked words that affect meaning.

café con azúcar	coffee with sugar
café sin azúcar	coffee without sugar
nunca	never
siempre	always
solo	only
hasta	until
todo el mundo	everybody
salvo / excepto	except
a causa de	because of

En mi familia todo el mundo bebe té sin leche.
In my family everyone drinks tea without milk.
Siempre meriendo galletas.
I always snack on biscuits in the afternoon.

Worked example

Read the texts about going to cafés.

Pablo: No suelo ir a las cafeterías porque los helados nunca son baratos. Prefiero tomar un té con amigos en mi casa.

Ana: Siempre voy a una cafetería con amigos para tomar un café y charlar con ellos. También comemos helados.

Miguel: Voy a la cafetería con mis hijos pero solamente los fines de semana. Mis hijos siempre comen el mismo helado: un helado de chocolate.

María: Como todo el mundo va a la cafetería, prefiero quedar con mis amigos para tomar un té o café en mi casa, ya que es más tranquilo. Además, odio los helados.

Complete the following sentence. Enter either **Pablo**, **Ana**, **Miguel** or **María**. .....Ana..... finds cafés sociable places.   **(1 mark)**

> To help you choose the correct answer, think about the negative alternative to words that you are looking for. For example:
> expensive ➡ not cheap ➡ nunca son baratos
> noisy café ➡ quiet house ➡ en mi casa … es más tranquilo
> not during the week ➡ at the weekend ➡ solamente los fines de semana

Now try this

Read the texts in the worked example again and complete the following sentences. You can use each person more than once.

(a) .... thinks the cafés are too noisy.   **(1 mark)**

(b) .... finds them good for children.   **(1 mark)**

(c) .... says that the ice creams they sell are expensive.   **(1 mark)**

(d) .... does not visit cafés during the week.   **(1 mark)**

(e) .... likes hot drinks but hates ice creams.   **(1 mark)**

Eating in a restaurant

Use this vocabulary to talk about eating out in restaurants.

Comer en un restaurante

la carta	menu
el plato del día	dish of the day
el menú del día	menu of the day
el menú a precio fijo	fixed price menu
la entrada	starter
el plato principal	main course
el postre	dessert
la cuenta	bill
el autoservicio	self service
el aperitivo	a drink (or food) before your meal

¿Quiere pan y mantequilla?
Would you like bread and butter?

Quiero …   I want …
- el bistec con patatas fritas.   steak and chips.
- el cordero con guisantes.   lamb with peas.

¡Buen provecho!   Enjoy your meal!

Using beber and comer in the preterite

	beber – to drink	comer – to eat
I	bebí	comí
he / she / it	bebió	comió
we	bebimos	comimos
they	bebieron	comieron

Para celebrar la Pascua comimos arroz con leche en un restaurante.

Worked example

Read this extract from *Una Madre* by Alejandro Palomas about a disappointing trip to a restaurant.

La verdad es que la elección del restaurante no pudo ser menos apropiada. A Silvia se le ocurrió que la mejor opción para la ocasión era el *Asador de las dos Castillas*, "un sitio estupendo donde se come de maravilla. Además, tiene un par de reservados (mesas) donde se está muy tranquilo. Yo me encargo de llamar. A los chicos de la oficina les encanta", dijo. "Luego, podríamos ir a alguna terraza a tomar el café", concedió.

El sitio resultó ser tranquilo, básicamente porque no había ni un *alma. El comedor olía a desinfectante de lavabos …

*alma = soul

Answer the following question **in English.**
What does the author say could not have been less appropriate?   (1 mark)

The choice of restaurant

Reading literary texts

✓ Don't expect to be able to translate everything in the text. You won't need to understand everything in order to answer the questions.

✓ Be prepared to scan the text to look for the answers. In the example, the phrase 'less appropriate' leads you to the first sentence of the text and the words just before menos apropiada give you the answer.

Now try this

Read the extract in the worked example again. Answer the following questions **in English.**

(a) What two reasons does Silvia give for choosing the *Asador*?   (2 marks)

(b) Who also recommended it?   (1 mark)

(c) What does she suggest for after the meal?   (1 mark)

(d) Was the restaurant busy? Give a reason for your answer.   (1 mark)

(e) What was the problem with the dining area?   (1 mark)

Shopping for food

Not many fruits and vegetables have similar names in Spanish, so learn them carefully!

¿Qué desea?

Deme ... , por favor.	Give me ... please.
¿Algo más?	Anything else?
Nada más.	Nothing else.
un melocotón	a peach
un plátano	a banana
unas frambuesas	raspberries
un albaricoque	an apricot
una ciruela	a plum
unas uvas	grapes
un pomelo	a grapefruit
una naranja	an orange
un pepino	a cucumber
una coliflor	a cauliflower
unas judías / alubias	beans
una lechuga	a lettuce

Quantities

In Spanish you use de (of) with quantities, even with grams and kilograms:

una lata de tomates	a tin of tomatoes
una barra de pan	a loaf of bread
una caja de galletas	a box of biscuits
una botella de agua	a bottle of water
un tarro de mermelada	a jar of marmalade
un paquete de caramelos	a bag of sweets
doscientos cincuenta gramos de ...	250 grams of ...
quinientos gramos de ...	500 grams of ...
medio kilo de ...	half a kilo of ...
un kilo de ...	1 kilo of ...
una docena de huevos	a dozen eggs

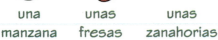

unas cerezas   una manzana   unas fresas   unas zanahorias

una piña   una cebolla   unos guisantes

To say 'a slice of ... ', you use una loncha de queso for 'a slice of cheese', but una rebanada de pan for 'a slice of bread'.

Worked example

🎧 LISTENING TRACK 21

Listen to the conversation in the grocery shop. Complete the sentence by putting a cross ✗ in the correct box. **(1 mark)**

The customer would like 500g of ...

☐ **A** cherries   ☐ **C** raspberries

☒ **B** strawberries   ☐ **D** apricots

Listen to the recording

– Hola, buenos días. ¿Qué desea?
– Deme quinientos gramos de fresas y ochocientos gramos de cerezas, por favor.

Exam alert

If you are not sure, have a guess to give you a chance of answering correctly. As well as learning fruits and vegetables, make sure you learn quantities and revise your numbers!

Now try this

🎧 LISTENING TRACK 22

Listen to the recording

Listen to the rest of the conversation in the worked example and complete each sentence by putting a cross ✗ in the correct box.

	A	B	C	D	
(a) The customer does not want any ...	☐ cherries	☐ strawberries	☐ pears	☐ apples	**(1 mark)**
(b) The shopkeeper has run out of ...	☐ beans	☐ plums	☐ grapes	☐ cucumber	**(1 mark)**
(c) The cost of the food purchased is ...	☐ 4,50€	☐ 6,50€	☐ 5,00€	☐ 14,50€	**(1 mark)**

Buying gifts

Be prepared to describe gifts, using colours and other adjectives.

Los regalos

los recuerdos	souvenirs
un reloj	a watch
el perfume	perfume
un póster	a poster
un cinturón	a belt
un sombrero	a hat
una gorra	a cap
una pelota	a ball
un videojuego	a computer game
una consola de juegos	a games console
unos calzoncillos	boxer shorts
una mochila	a backpack
una sudadera	a sweatshirt
unas zapatillas de deporte	trainers
de algodón	(made of) cotton
de cuero / de piel	(made of) leather
de lana	(made of) wool

Colours

verde negro amarillo rosa

rojo blanco marrón azul

Demonstrative adjectives

Grammar page 86

Demonstrative adjectives (this, that, these, those) are used with a noun and must agree with that noun.

	Masculine	Feminine
this / these		
Singular	este	esta
Plural	estos	estas
that / those		
Singular	ese	esa
Plural	esos	esas

este reloj	this watch
esta camiseta	this T-shirt

estas botas	esos zapatos
these boots	those shoes

Worked example

SPEAKING

You are in a clothes shop in Spain. The teacher will play the role of the shop assistant and will speak first.

Usted está en una tienda de ropa en un pueblo de España y quiere comprar algo.

1. Ropa – tipo
   Hola. ¿En qué puedo ayudarle?
   Me gustaría comprar una gorra.
2. Color preferido
   Muy bien. Tenemos varios colores. ¿Cuál prefiere?
   Prefiero una gorra roja.
3. !
   Habla bien el español. ¿De dónde es usted?
   Soy de Escocia.
4. Pueblo – opinión
   Muy bien. ¿Le gusta este pueblo?
   Sí, me gusta mucho porque es muy pintoresco y bastante pequeño.
5. ? Precio
   ¿Tiene una pregunta?
   ¿Cuánto cuesta la gorra?
   Son veinte euros.

Exam alert

Remember: when asked for an opinion in a role play, you need to justify your opinion!
Me gusta mucho porque es muy pintoresco y bastante pequeño.

This candidate has chosen to buy a cap for the gift. As **una gorra** is feminine, the colour needs to agree – **una gorra roja**. If the candidate had chosen a masculine item, such as a belt, it would have been **un cinturón rojo**.

Now try this

SPEAKING

Now prepare your own answers to the role play prompts in the worked example.

Opinions about food

Make sure you can give and understand opinions about food.

Opiniones sobre la comida

¿Qué tipo de comida te gusta?	What kind of food do you like?
Mi comida favorita es …	My favourite food is …
la comida española	Spanish food
la comida griega	Greek food
la comida india	Indian food
la comida italiana	Italian food
porque es …	because it's …
delicioso/a	delicious
graso/a	fatty
malo/a para la salud	unhealthy
nutritivo/a	nutritious
picante	spicy
rico/a	tasty
sabroso/a	tasty
salado/a	salty
sano/a	healthy

Using -ísimo for emphasis

Add -ísimo to the end of an adjective to make it stronger.

buenísimo/a	really good
riquísimo/a	really tasty

Expressing a range of opinions

Creo que …	I think that …
♥ Me gusta …	I like …
✗ No me gusta (nada) …	I don't like … (at all).
✗✗ Odio …	I hate …
En mi opinión …	In my opinion …

Creo que la comida española es buenísima.
I think Spanish food is really nice.
Odio las anchoas porque son saladas.
I hate anchovies because they are salty.

Don't forget to make adjectives agree!

Worked example

LISTENING TRACK 23

Listen to María talking about food and put a cross ✗ in the correct box. **(1 mark)**

In her restaurant María cooks …

 A Spanish food
☐ **B** Indian food
☐ **C** English food
☐ **D** Italian food

Listen to the recording

– ¡Hola! Me llamo María. Soy cocinera y trabajo en un restaurante español de Londres.

Listening strategies

✓ Be patient and continue to listen **carefully** even if the answers don't come up in the first few sentences.

✓ Remember that people don't always describe things directly. Listen out for **comparatives** and use these to work out opinions which aren't stated directly.

Listen to the recording

Now try this

LISTENING TRACK 24

Listen to the whole recording from the worked example and answer the following questions **in English**.

(a) What nationality is María's boyfriend? **(1 mark)**
(b) Why doesn't María cook at home? **(1 mark)**
(c) How does María describe the meals her boyfriend cooks? **(1 mark)**

The weather

Use this page to prepare for understanding weather forecasts.

¿Qué tiempo hace?

Llueve / Está lloviendo.

Nieva / Está nevando.

Hace sol.

Hay niebla.

Hace calor.

Hace frío.

Hace viento.	It's windy.
el pronóstico del tiempo	weather forecast
el clima	climate
Hace mal / buen tiempo.	It's bad / good weather.
Está nublado.	It's cloudy.
Hay tormenta.	It's stormy.
Hay truenos.	There's thunder.
Hay relámpagos.	There's lightning.
seco/a	dry
lluvioso/a	rainy
caluroso/a	hot
soleado/a	sunny

Different tenses

Understanding the weather in different tenses is a higher-level skill.

Expressions with hacer	
Hacía calor.	It was hot.
Hará frío.	It will be cold.
Hará sol.	It will be sunny.
Expressions with estar	
Estaba nublado.	It was cloudy.
Expressions with haber	
Había niebla.	It was foggy.
Habrá tormenta.	It will be stormy.
nevar (to snow) and llover (to rain)	
Nevaba.	It was snowing.
Llovía.	It was raining.
Va a nevar / llover.	It's going to snow / rain.

Look out for time markers as a clue to the tense.
ayer — yesterday
hoy — today
mañana — tomorrow

Worked example

TRACK 25

Listen to the weather forecast and put a cross ✗ in the correct box. **(1 mark)**

The forecast for Bilbao today is …

☐ **A** wind   ☐ **C** rain
☒ **B** sun   ☐ **D** snow

Listen to the recording

– Bilbao, sábado 12 de marzo. Ayer llovía, pero hoy hace sol. Mañana nevará.

Exam alert

You need to be secure with your verb tenses so that you can identify different time frames during a listening task.

The key word to listen out for here is **hoy** (today).

Listen to the recording

Now try this

TRACK 26

Listen to this forecast from the worked example and put a cross ✗ in the correct box for each question.

	A	B	C	D	
(a) In Seville yesterday it was …	☐ windy	☐ cold	☐ foggy	☐ snowing	**(1 mark)**
(b) It will be windy …	☐ tonight	☐ this morning	☐ tomorrow	☐ on Saturday	**(1 mark)**
(c) Now the weather is …	☐ hot	☐ stormy	☐ cloudy	☐ snowing	**(1 mark)**

Places to see

You need to know places in a town and you need prepositions to say where they are.

Los lugares de interés

Se puede ver ...	You can see ....
el ayuntamiento.	the town hall.
el museo.	the museum.
la galería de arte.	the art gallery.
el teatro.	the theatre.
el mercado.	the market.
la estación de tren.	the train station.
la iglesia.	the church.
la biblioteca.	the library.
la catedral.	the cathedral.
el castillo.	the castle.
el cine.	the cinema.
los monumentos.	the monuments.
Hay muchas tiendas.	There are lots of shops.
la carnicería	the butcher's
la pescadería	the fishmonger's
la panadería	the baker's
la frutería	the fruit shop
el supermercado	the supermarket
la ferretería	the hardware store
el quiosco (de periódicos)	the newspaper stand
la farmacia	the chemist's

Prepositions

Use prepositions to describe location.
Note that de + el changes to del.

Está ...

| delante de | detrás de | al lado de |
| in front of | behind | next to |

| entre | cerca de | lejos de |
| between | near to | far from |

enfrente de	opposite
a mano derecha / izquierda	on the right / left hand side
en la esquina	on the corner
a 10 minutos	10 minutes away

Está delante del cine.
It's in front of the cinema.

Worked example

Read Martín's note about what he has to do.

lunes
Ir al supermercado para comprar bolígrafos para el instituto. Llevar libros a la biblioteca delante del banco y comprar un regalo para José en la tienda del museo.

martes
Ir a la farmacia enfrente de la frutería a comprar perfume. Comprar entradas para la exposición de la galería de arte mañana. Mandar correo electrónico al banco. Por la noche comprar pan.

Complete the sentence below, using a word from the box.

| school | library | museum | bakery |
| supermarket | chemist's | gallery | bank |

To get ready for school Martín needs to buy equipment at the ..supermarket.. **(1 mark)**

Exam alert

When completing sentences using a box of words, make sure that you read ALL the statements in English carefully first. Then, after you have read the text, you can make your choice. In this case, most of the words could fit any sentence, so you need to understand some details in the text.

Now try this

Complete these sentences, using words from the box in the worked example. There are more words than gaps.

(a) Martín needs to buy a gift at the shop in the .... **(1 mark)**

(b) The first thing to do on Tuesday is buy something at the ....**(1 mark)**

(c) On Wednesday he will be going to the .... **(1 mark)**

(d) On Tuesday evening he will go to the .... **(1 mark)**

Had a look ☐   Nearly there ☐   Nailed it! ☐

Tourist information

Make sure you know the vocabulary for asking about tourist attractions.

En la oficina de turismo

¿Tiene … ?   Do you have … ?
un mapa de la región   a map of the region
una lista de hoteles   a list of hotels
una lista de albergues   a list of youth
  juveniles   hostels
un folleto de   a brochure about
  excursiones   trips
un horario de trenes /   a train / bus
  autobuses   timetable
Quiero información sobre …
I'd like information about …
una visita guiada (a pie)   a (walking) tour
¿Qué hay de interés en … ?
What is there of interest in … ?
¿A qué hora abre / cierra el museo?
What time does the museum open / close?
Hay …   There is …
Se puede …   It's possible …
Merece / Vale la pena ver … It's worth seeing …
Si yo fuera usted, visitaría …
If I were you, I would visit …
Lo interesante es que se puede …
The interesting thing is that you can …

Question words

Grammar page 103

¿Dónde?   Where?
¿Adónde?   Where to?
¿Cuánto?   How much?
¿Cuándo?   When?
¿A qué hora? At what time?
¿Qué?   What?
¿Cómo?   How?
¿Cuál?   Which?

lo + adjective

Use lo + adjective to refer to an abstract idea.
lo bueno   the good thing
lo malo   the bad thing
lo aburrido   the boring thing
lo interesante   the interesting thing

There is also a superlative form:
Lo más interesante es que hay playas bonitas.
The most interesting thing is the beautiful beaches.

Worked example

Translate this passage **into English**.   **(6 marks)**

Estoy de vacaciones en Costa Rica y las playas son tan bonitas. Fui a la oficina de turismo y …

I am on holiday in Costa Rica and the beaches are so beautiful. I went to the tourist information centre and …

Exam alert

You have to translate a passage from Spanish to English as part of the reading exam. You will be marked on communication and accuracy, so make sure that your translation communicates the meaning of the passage and that it flows well.

You often need to change the word order when translating so that your English text makes sense. For example, translate las playas bonitas as 'pretty beaches', not 'beaches pretty'!

Now try this

Translate the rest of the passage **into English**.   **(6 marks)**

… encontré mucha información, como por ejemplo, el horario de autobuses. Mañana me gustaría hacer una visita guiada a pie por el centro de la ciudad con mis padres.

Describing a town

This page will help you describe your town and talk about what you would like to change.

Descripción de mi ciudad

Mi ciudad se llama …	My town is called …
Está en el norte / este / sur / oeste de Inglaterra.	
It is in the north / east / south / west of England.	
Hay / Tiene doce mil habitantes.	
There are 12,000 inhabitants.	
En mi ciudad hay …	
In my town there is / are …	

muchos turistas.	lots of tourists.
muchas zonas de ocio.	lots of leisure areas.
una buena red de transporte público.	a good public transport network.
mucha contaminación.	lots of pollution.
muchos árboles.	lots of trees.
pocas tiendas de ropa.	few clothes shops.
pocas instalaciones.	few facilities.

En mi ciudad hay muchos espacios verdes.
In my town there are lots of green spaces.

The conditional tense

Grammar page 96

You use the conditional to talk about what you would do. To form it, add the following endings to the infinitive. Some verbs use a different stem, but the endings are the same for all verbs.

	hablar – to speak
I	hablaría
you	hablarías
he / she / it	hablaría
we	hablaríamos
you	hablaríais
they	hablarían

Construiría …	I would build …
Podría …	I would be able to …
Habría …	There would be …
Mejoraría …	I would improve …

Worked example

LISTENING TRACK 27

Listen to Héctor talking about his town.
Put a cross ✗ in **one** correct box.   **(1 mark)**

☐ **A** There are over 70,000 inhabitants.
☐ **B** Héctor would encourage more tourists to visit Gandía.
☐ **C** He would provide more green spaces.
☐ **D** Lanzarote has 150,000 inhabitants.
☐ **E** There are not enough buses in Lanzarote.
☐ **F** Laura thinks buses would improve daily life.
☐ **G** Looking after Lanzarote's natural resources is key.

Listen to the recording

– Vivo en Gandía, una ciudad que está en el sureste de España.

Listening strategies

✓ **Always** read the options before you listen. Identify key words and structures to listen out for.
✓ If you are confident of any answers on first listening, put a cross by those letters to reduce your options for the second listening.

Look at the sentences. What do you need to listen out for?
• Numbers (sesenta? no: setenta)
• Verbs in the conditional
• Key words: turistas, autobuses, espacios verdes, etc.

Now try this

LISTENING TRACK 28

Listen to the recording

Look at the worked example. Listen to the whole recording and put a cross ✗ in the other **three** correct boxes.   **(3 marks)**

Countries and nationalities

Remember to be accurate with your adjective endings when describing nationalities.

Países y nacionalidades

Soy de / Vivo en ...   I'm from / I live in ...

África / Asia / Europa   Africa / Asia / Europe

América del Norte /   North America
Norteamérica

América del Sur /   South America
Sudamérica

América Latina /   Latin America
Latinoamérica

España		español
Gran Bretaña		británico
Argentina		argentino
Japón		japonés
Irlanda		irlandés
Grecia		griego
Francia		francés
Alemania		alemán
Suiza		suizo
Venezuela		venezolano

Talking about nationalities

Like other adjectives, adjectives of nationality agree.

	Singular	Plural
Nationalities ending -o:		
Masculine	suiz**o**	suiz**os**
Feminine	suiz**a**	suiz**as**
Nationalities ending in a consonant:		
Masculine	inglé<u>s</u>	ingle**ses**
Feminine	ingle**sa**	ingle**sas**

When you talk about people from a country, you always use the definite article.
Me gustan los brasileños.
I like Brazilian people.

Nationalities with an accent on the ending lose it in feminine and plural forms, e.g.
escoc**és**   escoc**eses**   escoc**esa**

In Spanish, nationalities **don't** have a capital letter.

Worked example

Escribe a tu amigo/a en otro país sobre ti. **Debes** incluir los puntos siguientes:
• tu nacionalidad
• dónde naciste.   **(10 marks)**

Aiming Higher

Nací en México aunque desde hace diez años vivo en Estados Unidos porque mis padres trabajan aquí. Mi madre es venezolana pero se mudó a México con 15 años, así que soy mitad mexicano y mitad venezolano. Me gustan los colombianos, por lo tanto en el futuro viviré en Bogotá.

Aiming higher

✓ The best answer will use the bullet points to show off knowledge of a **range of tenses**. This candidate uses present, preterite and future to describe his nationality, and varies the **verb endings** to give information about his family too.
✓ Using **connectives** (aunque, porque, pero, así que, por lo tanto) makes your writing more coherent and more interesting.

Now try this

Write about your own nationality. Aim to write at least 40 words.   **(10 marks)**

Places to visit

This page gives more vocabulary for things to do in new places.

¿Qué vas a hacer?

Vamos a ir ...	Let's go ...
a la piscina municipal.	to the public swimming pool.
al cine.	to the cinema.
al campo.	to the countryside.
al centro histórico.	to the historic district.
al centro de ocio.	to the leisure centre.
al mercado.	to the market.
al parque de atracciones.	to the theme park.
al centro turístico costero.	to the seaside resort.
al parque zoológico.	to the zoo.

Se puede ...	You can ...
ver plazas y puentes.	see squares and bridges.
disfrutar de unas vistas maravillosas.	enjoy some marvellous views.
conocer la cultura.	experience the culture.
ver un espectáculo.	see a show.
ir a un partido.	go to a match.
ver exposiciones especiales.	see special exhibitions.

Using se puede to say what you can do

Se puede is an impersonal verb used to talk about what people in general can do. It is followed by the infinitive.

Se puede visitar
  un parque temático.
You can visit a theme park.
Se puede practicar muchos
  deportes.
You can do many sports.

Worked example

• ¿Qué lugares me recomendarías visitar como turista?

> Mi ciudad es muy interesante. Se puede visitar el museo y además hay muchos restaurantes y bares donde se puede comer tapas.

> Se puede visitar el museo y así se conoce la cultura. A mí me encanta Bilbao porque se puede experimentar la cultura vasca. También se puede caminar por el casco antiguo y se puede ver un espectáculo de música vasca porque forma parte de su patrimonio cultural. ¿Usted ha visitado el casco antiguo de Bilbao?

Exam alert

In the general conversation part of your speaking exam, make sure that you **justify** a **wide range** of individual thoughts and opinions. It is a good idea to ask the examiner questions, to show that you are able to **sustain** and **lead** the conversation.

Aiming higher

Try to include the following features:
- ✓ a connective (así, porque, pero, etc.) to make a complex sentence
- ✓ opinion phrases (en mi opinión, me encanta)
- ✓ less common verbs (to show a wider range of vocabulary)

Now try this

Now give your own answer to the question in the worked example.

Describing a region

Use this page to enable you to describe the region where you live.

Mi región

Mi región es tranquila. My region is quiet.

Mi barrio es ruidoso.

My neighbourhood is noisy.

La zona es residencial.   The area is residential.

El paisaje es bonito.   The scenery is beautiful.

Es una provincia industrial.

It's an industrial province.

Hay pocos habitantes.

There are not many inhabitants.

Vivo en las afueras de la ciudad.

I live in the suburbs.

Los alrededores son preciosos.

The surrounding area is beautiful.

Los bosques son pintorescos.

The woods are picturesque.

La torre fue construida hace doscientos años.

The tower was built two hundred years ago.

Antes había muchos bloques de pisos.

There used to be lots of tower blocks.

Ahora tiene más zonas verdes.

Now it has more green spaces.

Connectives

Use connectives to help you structure your opinions.

además	also, as well
por un lado …	on the one hand …
por otro lado …	on the other hand …
en realidad / de hecho	actually / in fact
aparte de	apart from
a pesar de esto	in spite of this
es decir	that is to say / I mean
sin duda	without a doubt

Parece una región histórica con muchos edificios impresionantes y, sin duda, es un lugar tranquilo.

It seems like a historic region with many impressive buildings and it is, without doubt, a peaceful area.

Worked example

Lee el artículo.

La provincia de Cádiz

El diverso carácter de la provincia de Cádiz está marcado por su gente, su bahía y su historia. En sus paisajes se aprecian grandes contrastes, desde el Campo de Gibraltar hasta la belleza de Jerez de la Frontera, sus pueblos blancos o las costas de Tarifa.

No se puede olvidar su capital, Cádiz, que tiene cultura y tradiciones que la diferencian del resto. Cádiz es sin duda el destino ideal para tus vacaciones.

En su costa atlántica destacan sus playas largas de arena fina. Muchas de ellas aún no están urbanizadas ni explotadas turísticamente.

Pon una cruz ✗ en la casilla correcta.   **(1 mark)**

El artículo dice que en la provincia hay …

☒ **A** playas y aldeas

☐ **B** bosques y montañas

☐ **C** muchas ciudades industriales

☐ **D** varios barrios ruidosos

Exam alert

Pon una cruz en la casilla correcta means 'Put a cross in the correct box'. Learn other key instructions too:

Escoge entre …

Choose between …

una palabra del recuadro de abajo

a word from the box below

Puedes usar palabras más de una vez.

You can use words more than once.

To choose the correct answer, rule out some options: woods and mountains are not mentioned, Cádiz is not described as industrial and pueblos are not described as noisy. Then make the connection between aldeas and pueblos.

Remember! Questions in Spanish require answers **in** Spanish.

Now try this

Lee el artículo y contesta las preguntas **en español**.

(a) Explica la diversidad de la provincia de Cádiz.   **(1 mark)**

(b) ¿Por qué se debe visitar la ciudad de Cádiz?   **(1 mark)**

School subjects

You need to be able to say what subjects you study, what you think of them and why.

Las asignaturas

Estudio ... I study ...

 el arte dramático

 el francés

 la geografía

 la música

 la tecnología

 el inglés

 la educación física

 la historia

 la informática

 el dibujo

 las matemáticas

 las ciencias

Giving opinions

Grammar page 101

- **me gusta** (I like) literally translates as 'it pleases me'.
- If the subject is plural, use **me gustan**.
- **me encanta** (I love) and **me interesa** (I'm interested in) work in the same way.

Me gusta la química. — I like chemistry.
Me encanta el español. — I love Spanish.
Me interesan las ciencias. — I'm interested in science.

Other ways to give your opinion:
Odio / Detesto — I hate
Encuentro — I find
Creo / Pienso — I think
Es / Son ... — It's / They're ...
interesante / fácil / útil / práctico/a
interesting / easy / useful / practical
difíciles / aburridos / inútiles / complicados
difficult / boring / useless / complicated

Worked example

LISTENING TRACK 29

Listen and put a cross ✗ in **one** correct box. **(1 mark)**
Marcela ...
☒ **A** enjoys studying languages
☐ **B** is unsure what to study next year
☐ **C** finds English more useful than French
☐ **D** likes French and English food

– Buenos días, señor director. Soy Marcela.
– Hola, Marcela, ¿qué te gustaría estudiar en enero?
– Me gustan mucho el inglés y el francés. Es muy útil estudiar idiomas.

Listen to the recording

Exam alert

Students often fail to link other words associated with a particular school subject with the word they have learned. For example, they don't connect química and física with las ciencias or relate acontecimientos pasados to la historia. Create a mind map for each school subject and add relevant vocabulary and phrases to help you learn this topic thoroughly.

Look out for other links: here, the inglés / francés link to languages is a useful one to spot.

Now try this

LISTENING TRACK 30

Listen to the recording

Look at the worked example. Listen to the whole recording and enter either **Marcela** or **Francisco** in the gaps below.

(a) .... thinks art is a waste of time. **(1 mark)**
(b) .... likes science. **(1 mark)**
(c) .... finds IT difficult. **(1 mark)**
(d) .... hates PE. **(1 mark)**

School life

Learn the vocabulary on this page to talk about your life in school.

La vida en el instituto

Presto atención en clase.	I pay attention in class.
Llevo mi bloc de notas.	I bring my pad of paper.
Repaso las asignaturas.	I revise my subjects.
Hago exámenes.	I do exams.
Escribo ensayos.	I write essays.
Corrijo los ejercicios.	I correct my exercises.
Contesto las preguntas de los profesores.	I answer the teachers.
Hablo con mis compañeros.	I talk to my classmates.
Saludo a mis amigos/as.	I say hi to my friends.
A veces me castigan.	I sometimes get detention.
No suspendo las pruebas.	I don't fail my tests.
Queremos aprobar el examen final.	We want to pass the final exam.
Voy al club de ciencias.	I go to science club.
Hacemos experimentos.	We do experiments.

Negatives

Grammar page 100

No (not) goes before the verb:
No voy al club de programación.
I don't go to coding club.
Los pasillos no están muy llenos.
The corridors are not very busy.

Other negatives go after a verb with no before it, or before the verb:
No copio nunca de la pizarra.
I never copy from the board.
Nunca usamos libros de texto.
We never use textbooks.
No hay nadie en la sala de profesores.
There is no one in the staff room.
Nadie repitió un año.
No one repeated a year.
No … ni … means 'not (either) … or …'
No estudio sociología ni periodismo.
I don't study sociology or media studies.

Worked example

Traduce las frases siguientes **al español**.
(a) I always do my homework. **(2 marks)**
Siempre hago mis deberes.
(b) I talk with my classmates during break. **(2 marks)**
Hablo con mis compañeros durante el recreo.
(c) Last week I worked hard in maths. **(3 marks)**
La semana pasada trabajé duro en matemáticas.
(d) I don't like revising my subjects but it's important. **(3 marks)**

No me gusta repasar mis materias pero es importante.

Exam alert

When translating into Spanish, you will be marked on accuracy and communication. To answer successfully, you need to check that your verbs are in the correct tense and have the correct person ending.

All the verbs are in the correct tenses and use the correct endings: hago, hablo, trabajé, no me gusta repasar, es. Make sure your other vocabulary is accurate, too: in la semana pasada, pasada ends in -a because semana is a feminine noun.

Now try this

Traduce las frases siguientes **al español**.
(a) I never talk to my friends in class. **(2 marks)**
(b) I sometimes read books in the library. **(2 marks)**
(c) Yesterday morning I wrote a history essay. **(3 marks)**
(d) I prefer talking to the teacher because I hate copying from the board. **(3 marks)**

The school day

You need to be able to describe your school routine.

El día en el instituto

Voy al instituto en tren.
I go to school by train.

Llego a las ocho y cuarto.
I arrive at quarter past eight.

Las clases empiezan a las nueve menos veinte.
Classes start at twenty to nine.

Como algo durante el recreo.
I eat something during break.

El descanso para almorzar dura cincuenta minutos.
The lunch break lasts fifty minutes.

Las clases terminan a las tres y media.
Classes finish at three thirty.

Entreno en el equipo de bádminton del instituto.
I train for the school badminton team.

Después del instituto trabajo en una tienda.
After school I work in a shop.

¿Qué hora es?

midday = mediodía
midnight = medianoche

en punto

menos cinco   y cinco

menos diez   y diez

menos cuarto   y cuarto

menos veinte   y veinte

menos veinticinco   y veinticinco

y media

a.m. = de la mañana   p.m. = de la tarde / de la noche

Worked example

Read José's text about his school day.

En invierno voy al instituto en autobús porque hace mucho frío. Normalmente llego a las nueve menos veinte y voy directamente al patio para charlar con mis amigos. Las clases empiezan a las nueve y lo malo es que solo tenemos quince minutos de recreo durante la mañana. El descanso para almorzar también es muy corto porque empieza a las doce y termina a la una menos cuarto. Las clases terminan a las tres y cuarto pero siempre voy a algo antes de volver a casa.

Answer the question **in English**.

What does José do first when he gets to school? **(1 mark)**
He goes to chat with his friends in the playground.

Reading strategies

Remember that you are not going to find an exact translation of the information requested by the question. You need to deduce meaning and think about how information can be conveyed in different ways.

Here, you will not find the word 'first', **primero**, in the text. Instead, look for what José describes after his arrival at school: **llego a las nueve menos veinte y ...** . The word **directamente** shows that he does not do anything else before going to the playground. If you cannot remember the word **patio**, you could guess where you might talk with your friends before school, ruling out any vocabulary you can remember, such as **clase** or **comedor**.

Now try this

Read the text in the worked example again and answer the following questions **in English**.

(a) What is not good about morning break?   **(1 mark)**

(b) How long does lunch last?   **(1 mark)**

(c) How do you know José does not go home at 3.15p.m.?   **(1 mark)**

Comparing schools

Be prepared to compare Spanish schools with schools in your own country.

Mi instituto, tu instituto

En España …	In Spain …
hay menos exámenes.	there are fewer exams.
no estudian ciertas asignaturas.	they do not study certain subjects.
las vacaciones son más largas.	the holidays are longer.
la jornada escolar es más corta.	the school day is shorter.
no comen en el instituto.	they don't eat lunch at school.
los estudiantes llaman a sus profesores por su nombre.	students call their teachers by their first name.

Los alumnos no tienen que llevar uniforme.
Students do not have to wear uniform.

Aiming higher

Avoid using me gusta and odio all the time – stand out from the crowd by using something more impressive …

No lo aguanto. I can't stand it.	No lo aguantaba. I couldn't stand it.
No lo soporto. I can't bear it.	No lo soportaba. I couldn't bear it.
No me importa. It's not important to me.	No me importaba. It was not important to me.
Me enoja. It annoys me.	Me enojaba. It annoyed me.
No es justo. It's not fair.	No era justo. It wasn't fair.
Me da igual … I'm not bothered about …	Me daba igual … I wasn't bothered about …

Worked example

¿Qué diferencias hay entre los institutos en España y en Inglaterra?

Los colegios en España son diferentes de los colegios ingleses. Los alumnos no llevan uniforme y en algunos colegios las clases terminan más tarde que en el mío. Las vacaciones son más largas: casi tres meses. ¡Me gustaría tener estas vacaciones en mi colegio!

Aiming Higher

En Inglaterra los alumnos llevan uniforme y no me gusta mucho, pero visité un instituto español durante un intercambio y ¡qué sorpresa! los alumnos españoles no tenían que llevarlo. ¡Qué envidia! ¡No es justo! Lo que no me da envidia es su horario. Los alumnos en el colegio que visité tienen clase hasta las cinco de la tarde. No me gustaría eso.

Aiming higher

Try working in expressions like these:
No es justo que …
It's not fair that …
¡Ojalá pudiera tener más vacaciones!
If only I could have more holidays!

- Use of other tenses (visité) adds sophistication to this answer.
- **Exclamation phrases** are also useful to show opinions.
- Using more interesting opinions (¡No es justo!) makes the language more complex, as does the inclusion of a conditional: no me gustaría (I wouldn't like).

Now try this

Habla de las diferencias entre los institutos en España y en Inglaterra.

Try to include some different information and express a preference.

53

Describing schools

Use this page to learn vocabulary for describing your school facilities and activities.

Mi instituto

En la cartera tengo ...
In my school bag I have ...

un estuche.	a pencil case.
unos lápices.	some pencils.
unas tijeras.	scissors.
un sacapuntas.	a sharpener.
bolígrafo.	a pen.
(barra de) pegamento.	glue (stick).
unos cuadernos.	some exercise books.

En mi instituto de enseñanza secundaria hay ...
In my secondary school there is/are ...

una cantina.	a canteen.
unos vestuarios.	some changing rooms.
muchas aulas.	lots of classrooms.
un gimnasio.	a gymnasium.
un laboratorio de idiomas.	a language lab.
un despacho.	a school office.

No tenemos autobús escolar.
We don't have a school bus.
No hay campo de deporte.
There is no sports field.

Using the verb tener in different tenses

Tener (to have) is a verb you need to know. Be ready to use it in different tenses. It is a radical-changing verb (note the vowel change in the present).

	Present	Preterite	Future
I	tengo	tuve	tendré
you	tienes	tuviste	tendrás
he/she/it	tiene	tuvo	tendrá
we	tenemos	tuvimos	tendremos
you (pl.)	tenéis	tuvisteis	tendréis
they	tienen	tuvieron	tendrán

El año pasado tuvimos que llevar una calculadora a todas las clases de matemáticas.
Last year we had to bring a calculator to all our maths lessons.

Worked example

Describe tu instituto. **Debes** incluir los puntos siguientes:
* cómo es
* tu opinión
* algunos cambios recientes.   **(15 marks)**

No me gusta mucho mi instituto, es muy viejo y bastante pequeño. No hay biblioteca y hay pocos ordenadores, así que es difícil hacer los deberes. Construyeron una piscina el año pasado. Desafortunadamente no me gusta nada nadar.

This student has done well to include opinions as well as introducing the **preterite tense** but a greater **variety** of vocabulary and tenses would be needed for a higher-level answer.

Aiming Higher

Mi instituto es grande y moderno y tiene muchas instalaciones, por eso me gusta mucho. No tenemos muchas instalaciones deportivas, así que van a construir una nueva pista de atletismo. Tenemos también aulas nuevas porque el año pasado se construyeron nuevos edificios.

This answer includes more detail. Using a passive form like se construyeron also shows that you know, and can use, a wider range of structures accurately.

Now try this

Write your own answer to the writing task in the worked example. Write approximately 60 words.   **(15 marks)**

School rules

This page will help you talk about school rules and what you think of them.

Las normas del instituto

En mi instituto ...	In my school ...
No se puede ...	You can't ...
Está prohibido ...	It is forbidden to ...
No se debe ...	You shouldn't ...
llevar maquillaje	wear make-up
usar el móvil en clase	use your phone in class
masticar chicle	chew gum
mandar mensajes	send messages
llegar tarde	arrive late
correr por los pasillos	run in the corridors
ser antipático	be unpleasant
hablar mientras habla el profesor	talk while the teacher is talking

No se debe ser ni vago ni grosero.
You shouldn't be either lazy or rude.

Son tontas / necesarias / anticuadas / útiles / inútiles.
They are stupid / necessary / old fashioned / useful / useless.

Key verbs + the infinitive

	querer – want	poder – be able to	deber – should, ought to
I	quiero	puedo	debo
you	quieres	puedes	debes
he / she / it	quiere	puede	debe
we	queremos	podemos	debemos
you	queréis	podéis	debéis
they	quieren	pueden	deben

Quiere llevar pendientes pero no se puede llevar joyas.
She wants to wear earrings but you can't wear jewellery.

Worked example

¿Existen normas en tu instituto?

En mi instituto tengo que llevar uniforme.
Odio el uniforme porque es incómodo.
En mi opinión, las normas son anticuadas.
Son tontas e inútiles pero algunas personas
piensan que son necesarias. ¡Qué horror!

Aiming Higher

En mi instituto, hay muchas normas. Acaban
de introducir una nueva y ahora no se
permite usar el móvil en clase. ¡No es justo!
Hay que dejarlo en casa, o apagarlo antes
de entrar en el instituto. Creo que los
profesores son demasiado estrictos.

> Use a variety of opinion words and adjectives (incómodo, anticuadas, inútiles) to say not only what you think, but also what others think – this will help you to aim for a higher grade.

> Use idiomatic phrases such as acaban de. They add variety to your language and make it sound more sophisticated. Try adding an exclamation phrase as well (¡Qué horror!).

Now try this

Answer this question. Speak for about one minute.
• ¿Existen normas en tu instituto?

> Try to include:
> • three opinions / adjectives
> • three connectives
> • three different phrases with the infinitive
> • a Spanish exclamation.

Problems at school

Use this page to talk about the pressures and problems you face at school.

Los problemas en el instituto

Tienes que ...   You have to ...
  respetar a todo el mundo.   respect everyone.
  sacar buenas notas.   get good grades.
  aprobar los exámenes.   pass exams.
  tener buenas   have good
    cualificaciones.   qualifications.
  mejorar tu rendimiento.   improve your
      performance.
  pensar en el futuro.   think about the
      future.

No se debería ...   You should not ...
  acosar / intimidar.   bully.
  reñir.   quarrel.
  pelear.   fight.
  molestar.   annoy.
  hacer novillos.   bunk lessons.
Hay mucha presión.   There is a lot of
      pressure (to achieve
      good marks).

el boletín de notas   school report
la vuelta al instituto   the first day back
      at school

The personal 'a'

When the direct object of a verb is a person, you add a before the person. This is not translated into English.

Miguel intimida a otros alumnos.
Miguel intimidates other pupils.

No se debería insultar a los demás.
You should not insult other people.

el acoso escolar	bullying
estresante	stressful
débil	weak
torpe	clumsy
grosero	rude

Worked example

LISTENING TRACK 31

Listen to the start of a conversation about problems at school. What problem is mentioned? Put a cross ✗ in **one** correct box. **(1 mark)**
☐ A bullying
☒ B pressure to do well
☐ C no free time
☐ D messy environment
☐ E timetable problems
☐ F journey to school
☐ G fighting in the playground

Listen to the recording

– Yo tengo miedo de no aprobar los exámenes. Mis padres esperan mucho de mí.

Exam alert

Avoid common errors such as just listening for one or two specific words. Think about all possible words that may be applicable for each category. So for bullying, don't just focus on acoso but listen for intimidar (to intimidate), insultar (to insult), molestar (to annoy), pelearse (to fight), una pelea (a fight), etc.

In this question you do not hear the word **presión**, but instead the pressure is explained with **tengo miedo de no aprobar** (I am afraid of not passing) and **mis padres esperan mucho de mí** (my parents expect a lot from me).

Now try this

LISTENING TRACK 32

Listen to the recording

Look at the worked example. Listen to the rest of the conversation and put a cross ✗ in the other **two** correct boxes. **(2 marks)**

Primary school

Use the imperfect tense to describe what you did at primary school.

La escuela de educación primaria

Cuando tenía diez años era travieso.
When I was 10, I was naughty.
Iba a una escuela de primaria cerca de mi casa.
I used to go to a primary school near my house.
Tenía menos amigos.
I used to have fewer friends.
Jugaba solamente con mis amigas.
I only used to play with my female friends.
Comía los bocadillos que mi abuelo me preparaba.
I used to eat sandwiches that my grandfather prepared.
No estudiaba español.   I didn't study Spanish.

Hacía más deporte.
I used to do more sport.

The imperfect tense

Grammar page 94

The imperfect tense is used to describe what **used to happen** or what **was happening**.
It is formed as follows:

hablar to speak	comer to eat	vivir to live
hablaba	comía	vivía
hablabas	comías	vivías
hablaba	comía	vivía
hablábamos	comíamos	vivíamos
hablabais	comíais	vivíais
hablaban	comían	vivían

Exam strategies

Learn tenses by chanting them – hablaba, hablabas, hablaba ... Start off by reading them, then close your book and see how many you can chant without looking. Keep going until you can do the whole verb.

Worked example

Escribe sobre tu vida escolar. **Debes** incluir el punto siguiente:
- tus experiencias de la escuela primaria.   **(10 marks)**

Aiming Higher   Cuando tenía diez años era travieso y la escuela primaria era aburrida. Estudiaba muchas asignaturas y muchos idiomas. La lengua que más me gustaba era el francés. De pequeño, estaba más contento porque tenía más amigos. La vida era más fácil, no tenía tantos deberes y los profesores eran menos severos.

Exam alert

Make sure that your writing is clear and legible. You will not be successful if the examiner cannot read your writing and therefore cannot grade your communication or accuracy.

Aiming higher

- ✓ Including **imperfect** tense verbs shows a confident and secure use of a tense.
- ✓ Use a **variety** of vocabulary (here, idiomas / lengua).
- ✓ An **opinion** phrase in the imperfect (me gustaba) is always a good addition.

Now try this

Escribe sobre tus experiencias de la escuela primaria. Escribe aproximadamente 50 palabras **en español**. **(10 marks)**

Success in school

Use this page to learn vocabulary for describing school achievements.

Tener éxito en el colegio

Para tener éxito …	To be successful …
es importante …	it is important …
es necesario …	it is necessary …
escuchar bien	to listen well
hacer preguntas	to ask questions
llevarte bien con otros	to get on well with others
mejorar tus notas	to improve your grades
estar motivado/a	to be motivated
organizar tu tiempo	to organise your time
aprovechar las oportunidades	to take advantage of opportunities
dormir bien	to sleep well
desarrollar buenos hábitos de estudio	to develop good studying habits
no dejar todo para último momento	not to leave everything to the last minute

Expressing obligation or necessity

You can use tener que + infinitive:
Tenemos que estudiar mucho.
We have to study a lot.

You can also use hay que + infinitive:
Para tener éxito hay que hacer buen uso de tu agenda.
To be successful you have to make good use of your planner/diary.

Or you can use phrases such as es importante, es necesario, es esencial, es obligatorio + infinitive:
Es esencial no perder tiempo.
It is essential not to waste time.

Es necesario encontrar un lugar cómodo y tranquilo para hacer los deberes.
You have to find a comfortable and quiet place to do your homework.

Worked example

READING

Read the article.

Cómo ser un estudiante exitoso

Ir al colegio todos los días es muy importante si quieres sacar buenas notas, pero hay otro tipo de atributos que también son necesarios para ser un estudiante de éxito. Lo primero, es fundamental evitar las distracciones. Esto puede resultar difícil pero es muy importante. Apaga siempre el móvil cuando estás haciendo los deberes. En segundo lugar, hacer bien los deberes en casa y prestar atención en clase siempre van a dar buenos resultados. Cuando termines el colegio habrás sacado buenas notas y tendrás la motivación necesaria para el siguiente paso de tu vida. Cuanto antes te conviertas en un estudiante de éxito, mejor será tu vida futura. Vas a necesitar paciencia, motivación y tenacidad.

Answer the question **in English**.
What is difficult to manage but essential for success?   **(1 mark)**
Avoiding distractions

Exam alert

Many higher level texts will contain vocabulary that you have not met before. You are not expected to understand each and every word. However, you are expected to be able to work out the sense of the passage, and you will succeed in answering the questions if you have revised your vocabulary adequately.

In this text, although there are complex constructions, there are also lots of cognates which help you decode the passage: atributos (attributes), distracciones (distractions), motivación (motivation), etc.

Now try this

READING

Read the article in the worked example again and answer the following questions **in English**.

(a) How can you avoid distractions at home?   **(1 mark)**
(b) What **two** things always lead to good results?   **(2 marks)**
(c) What characteristics will you have to possess? Name one.   **(1 mark)**

School trips

Learn vocabulary and structures to help you describe your school trips.

Una excursión del colegio

Fuimos a ...	We went to ...

durante las vacaciones de mitad de trimestre
during half term

Practicamos el español / francés / mandarín.
We practised Spanish / French / Mandarin.

Nuestro profesor de español nos acompañó.
Our Spanish teacher accompanied us.

Aprendimos mucho.   We learned a lot.

Disfrutamos de un día especial.
We enjoyed a special day.

Visitamos el museo.   We visited the museum.

Conocimos el parque.   We got to know the park.

Hicimos unas actividades culturales.
We did some cultural activities.

Fue una experiencia divertida.
It was an enjoyable experience.

Using a variety of tenses

✓ You can say what you **normally** do on trips:
Normalmente vamos a un museo.
Normally we go to a museum.

✓ Say what you did **on a recent trip**:
Fuimos al cine para ver una película japonesa.
We went to the cinema to see a Japanese film.

✓ Say what you **used to** do on past trips:
En la escuela primaria las excursiones eran más cortas.
In primary school trips used to be shorter.

✓ Say what you **will** do for your next trip:
Aprenderemos mucho español.
We will learn a lot of Spanish.

Worked example

Read the article.
Complete the sentence by putting a cross ✗ in the correct box.   **(1 mark)**

Children love school trips because ...
- ☐ **A** they don't have to get up early.
- ☐ **B** they love being with their friends.
- ☐ **C** they like seeing teachers out of the classroom.
- ☒ **D** they feel as if it is a day off from their studies.

Don't worry if there is a lot of unfamiliar vocabulary! If you know some of this topic vocabulary, you can work out that the answer is D from **no tienen que ir al colegio**.

Las excursiones escolares

A los niños les encantan las excursiones porque no tienen que ir al colegio, sentarse en clase a leer y escribir o escuchar a la profesora durante horas. Nosotros los profesores sabemos que llevar a los niños de excursión tiene muchas ventajas. En las excursiones los niños aprenden a relacionarse entre sí de una manera más positiva: mientras van en el autobús o durante la hora de la comida. Es posible que hasta hablen con niños que no forman parte de su grupo habitual de amigos. Algunos de los tipos de excursiones más populares son las visitas a los museos, las bibliotecas, las granjas o los zoos. Lo mejor de las excursiones es que los niños pueden visitar lugares que son completamente nuevos para ellos y esto es enriquecedor porque expande sus mentes y les permite entrar en contacto con mundos y realidades distintas.

Now try this

Read the article in the worked example again and put a cross ✗ in the correct box to complete each statement.

		A	B	C	D	
(a)	The benefits are ...	☐ clear to teachers	☐ not many	☐ surprising	☐ not educational	**(1 mark)**
(b)	A trip to a ... is not mentioned.	☐ zoo	☐ museum	☐ market	☐ farm	**(1 mark)**
(c)	The best thing is visiting ... places.	☐ interesting	☐ exciting	☐ new	☐ beautiful	**(1 mark)**

School events

Revise vocabulary for describing events that take place at your school.

Las eventos en el instituto

un concurso de talentos   a talent show

un campeonato de remo

a rowing championship

muchos torneos de fútbol

lots of football tournaments

un partido de balonmano

a handball match

una obra de teatro   a play

un concierto de la orquesta del instituto

a school orchestra concert

la fiesta de fin de curso   the end-of-year party

una reunión con el orientador

a meeting with the careers adviser

> Recaudamos fondos para nuestra área de recreo.
> We are fundraising for our playground.

Desde hace and desde

Use desde hace ('for') to say how long you have been doing something. It is used with the **present** tense of the verb.

Canto en el coro desde hace dos años.
I have been singing in the choir for two years.

Nuestro instituto participa en el concurso de ortografía desde hace cinco años.
Our school has been taking part in the spelling competition for five years.

Use desde ('since') to say when you started doing something. It is also used with the **present** tense of the verb.

Entrenamos para el partido desde marzo.
We have been training for the match since March.

Worked example

Listen to the head teacher's speech and answer the question **in English**.

Why was it such a successful year for school sport? Give **two** reasons.

(2 marks)

Listen to the recording

basketball team won eight out of ten matches / school won five gold karate medals

> El equipo de baloncesto ha ganado ocho de los últimos diez partidos y los participantes en el campeonato regional de kárate han vuelto con cinco medallas de oro.

Exam alert

Pay attention to the number of marks available. Where there are two marks, you will need to give two pieces of information. The instruction will always be highlighted in bold where this is required, so make sure you read the instructions carefully.

> To answer this question successfully, you need to identify the activity and ALSO what they won. Therefore you need to pick out numbers too: ocho de los últimos diez and cinco medallas de oro.

Now try this

Listen to the recording

Listen to the rest of the speech from the worked example and answer the following questions **in English**.

(a) What other achievement is mentioned in the speech? **(1 mark)**

(b) Which event does the head teacher mention as being her favourite? **(1 mark)**

(c) Who does she congratulate? **(1 mark)**

School exchanges

Use this page to learn how to talk about exchange visits.

Los intercambios

Nos ayudan a ...   They help us to ...
Te permiten ...   They allow you to ...
viajar a / conocer otro país
travel to / get to know another country
aprender de otras culturas y costumbres
learn about other cultures and customs
entender más fácilmente / dominar otros idiomas
understand other languages more easily / speak other languages well
vivir una gran aventura
experience a great adventure
experimentar algo nuevo
experience something new
Tienen beneficios incalculables para tu futuro.
They have invaluable benefits for your future.

¿Qué hiciste?

Estuve con una familia.   I stayed with a family.
Hice nuevos amigos.   I made new friends.
Fui a clase de distintas asignaturas.
I attended different lessons.
Vi el mundo de forma diferente.
I saw the world differently.
Hice varias actividades culturales.
I did some cultural activities.
Fui a dos excursiones.
I went on two trips.
El intercambio duró una semana.
The exchange lasted a week.
Creé entradas en el blog del intercambio.
I wrote entries for the exchange blog.

Comí platos típicos.

Worked example

SPEAKING

Topic: Cultural life
Mira la foto y prepara las respuestas a los siguientes puntos:
- la descripción de la foto
- tu opinión sobre los intercambios
- un intercambio o una excursión cultural que hiciste
- tus planes para aprender más de otras culturas
- !

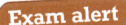

En esta foto hay un grupo de estudiantes ingleses que hacen un intercambio en España. Han visitado el centro histórico de la ciudad. A mí me encantan los intercambios porque te permiten hacer nuevos amigos de otro país. El año pasado estuve con una familia muy amable de Madrid. Aprendí mucho español y fue muy interesante ir al instituto. En el futuro me gustaría ir a Sudamérica. Quiero aprender más de la cultura latinoamericana. Los intercambios son importantes porque nos ayudan a conocer otros países y a dominar otros idiomas.

Exam alert

In the picture-based discussion, the examiner will ask you a question for each of the bullet points. For both tiers, there are five bullet points. For the Higher tier, the last one is an unexpected question (!).

The examiner's questions would be:
1. Describe la foto.
2. ¿Te gustan los intercambios?
3. ¿Has hecho algún intercambio o alguna excursión cultural para mejorar tu español?
4. ¿Te gustaría aprender más de otras culturas?
5. ¿Por qué son importantes los intercambios?
This candidate uses a range of tenses and some complex vocabulary to answer each point.

Now try this

SPEAKING

Prepare your own answers to the picture-based discussion in the worked example above.

Future plans

Using the future tense and the subjunctive to talk about future plans will make your writing and speaking more natural.

Tus planes para el futuro

Cuando sea mayor ...	When I'm older ...
Cuando termine la universidad / mi aprendizaje ...	When I finish university / my apprenticeship ...
Trabajaré como ...	I'll work as ...
Trabajaré en el extranjero.	I'll work abroad.
Haré trabajo voluntario.	I'll do voluntary work.
Viviré con mis amigos.	I'll live with my friends.
Viajaré mucho.	I'll travel a lot.
Seré famoso/a.	I'll be famous.
Ganaré mucho dinero.	I'll earn lots of money.
Seré muy feliz.	I will be very happy.
Me casaré y tendré hijos.	I'll get married and have children.
Es un campo en el que me gustaría trabajar.	It's a field in which I would like to work.

The subjunctive

Grammar page 99

The subjunctive is used after cuando to talk about an event in the future.
To form the subjunctive, replace the infinitive ending with the following:

hablar to speak	comer to eat	vivir to live
hable	coma	viva
hables	comas	vivas
hable	coma	viva
hablemos	comamos	vivamos
habléis	comáis	viváis
hablen	coman	vivan

> Cuando tenga veinte años, viajaré mucho. When I'm 20, I'll travel a lot.

Worked example

SPEAKING

- ¿Cuáles son tus planes para el futuro?

  No sé qué voy a hacer después de los exámenes. Me gustaría trabajar en el extranjero porque me encanta visitar nuevos lugares.

Aiming Higher

  Cuando sea mayor y termine la universidad, viajaré mucho. Ganaré mucho dinero, así que seré feliz porque podré comprar mucha ropa.

> - Use the future tense (viajaré, ganaré) to say what you will do.
> - Use connectives (así que, porque) to justify your opinions and to create more impressive sentences.
> - There is a good example of how to use cuando + the subjunctive to add variety to what you say.

Now try this

SPEAKING

Answer this question. Speak for about one minute.
- ¿Cuáles son tus planes para el futuro?

> Try to include:
> - one or two subjunctive phrases
> - two or three future tense phrases
> - an opinion phrase.

Future education plans

Use ir with the infinitive to talk about what you're going to do when you finish school.

Qué hacer en el futuro

el año que viene / el año próximo	next year
en el futuro	in the future
No estoy seguro/a.	I'm not sure.
Si saco buenas notas …	If I get good grades …
Voy a …	I'm going to …
estudiar lenguas / idiomas	study languages
ir a la universidad	go to university
buscar / encontrar empleo	look for / find a job
hacer un aprendizaje	do an apprenticeship
tener éxito	be successful

seguir estudiando en el instituto
continue studying in my school

ir a otro instituto para alumnos de 16 a 18 años
go to a sixth-form college

ganar mucho dinero
earn lots of money

Immediate future tense

This form of the future (using ir + infinitive) is like the English 'going to', and is used to express plans and intentions.

Grammar page 95

I	voy		ir
you	vas		buscar
he / she / it	va	a	hacer
we	vamos		seguir
you	vais		trabajar
they	van		estudiar

Voy a ir a la universidad.
I'm going to go to university.

Va a estudiar música.
He is going to study music.

Worked example

Escribe un texto sobre tu instituto. **Debes** incluir el punto siguiente: **(10 marks)**
• Tus planes para el futuro.

El año que viene voy a estudiar idiomas porque me encanta el alemán. No es fácil pero es interesante.

Quiero seguir estudiando el año próximo. Me gustaría estudiar idiomas porque me encanta saber más de otras culturas. Es más, el año pasado saqué buenas notas en alemán. Si sigo sacando buenas notas en el futuro, iré a la universidad porque quiero ser traductora en la Unión Europea.

Aiming higher

✓ **Vary** your tenses – this makes your answer more interesting and lets you show off what you know.

✓ **Develop** your answer – always look for opportunities to add more information, e.g. Es más, el año pasado saqué buenas notas …
What's more, last year I got good marks.

✓ Make it **stand out** – an unusual twist will help distinguish it, e.g. quiero ser traductora en la Unión Europea.
I want to be a translator in the European Union.

✓ **Impress** with interesting structures:
Si sigo sacando buenas notas en el futuro, iré … If I keep getting good grades in the future, I will go … .

Now try this

Write about your future plans. Write at least 30–40 words.

(10 marks)

Using languages

Use this page to help you talk about the importance of learning another language.

Los idiomas

Vivimos en una sociedad global.
We live in a global society.
Aprender otro idioma es importante porque puedes …
Learning another language is important because you can …

mejorar tu carrera.	improve your career.
conseguir un trabajo más fácilmente.	find a job more easily.
obtener un mejor salario.	get a better salary.
trabajar como traductor(a).	work as a translator.
disfrutar mejor tus viajes.	enjoy your trips more.
comunicarte mejor en otros países.	communicate better in other countries.
entender más del mundo.	understand more about the world.
conocer más gente.	get to know more people.
mejorar tu memoria.	improve your memory.

Aiming higher

Learn as many verbs as you can. They will help elevate your language and make it easier to express more abstract ideas. Make your own list of exciting verbs that can be used across different topic areas. For each verb, write an example for the first person (yo) in a different tense. Watch out for the irregular verbs!

Infinitive	mejorar (reg) to improve	obtener (irreg) to obtain
Preterite	mejoré	obtuve
Present	mejoro	obtengo
Near future	voy a mejorar	voy a obtener
Future	mejoraré	obtendré

Worked example

Read the article.
Answer the question **in English**.
Where is Spanish the official language?   **(1 mark)**

in more than 20 countries

You will not find a long list of countries in the text, but instead a sentence which says where you can travel with Spanish: **se habla en más de 20 países**.

¿Por qué estudiar español? 🇪🇸

Hoy en día es necesario aprender un segundo idioma. Aprender español es tanto útil como divertido. ¿Por qué? Hay varias razones de peso:

- El español es muy útil a la hora de viajar, se habla en más de 20 países donde es la lengua oficial.
- El español es un idioma clave para los negocios en EEUU y en muchas partes del mundo.
- Aprender otra lengua, como el español, te puede ayudar a conocer mejor tu propio idioma y además te puede facilitar aprender otros idiomas distintos.

Y por si todavía necesitas encontrar razones para aprender el español: según un estudio del Instituto Cervantes, más de 500 millones de personas hablan español, esto representa más del 6% de la población mundial. Además, después del chino, el español es el segundo idioma mas hablado del mundo y el segundo más utilizado después del inglés. Se cree que para el año 2030 el 7.5% de la población mundial hablará español.

Now try this

Read the article again from the worked example and answer these questions **in English**.

(a) Give **two** reasons why learning Spanish is useful.   **(2 marks)**

(b) What do six per cent of the world's population do?   **(1 mark)**

(c) Which language is most widely spoken in the world?   **(1 mark)**

(d) Spanish is becoming more popular. How do you know this?   **(1 mark)**

Jobs

Use this page to help you talk about the different jobs people do.

Empleos

un/a abogado/a	a lawyer
un/a actor/actriz	an actor
un/a agente de policía / un/a policía	a police officer
un/a agricultor/a	a farmer
un/a auxiliar de vuelo / un/a azafato/a	an airline cabin crew member
un/a arquitecto/a	an architect
un/a bombero/a	a firefighter
un/a cajero/a	a cashier
un/a camarero/a	a waiter
un/a cocinero/a	a cook
un/a constructor/a	a builder
un/a dentista	a dentist
un/a enfermero/a	a nurse
un/a fontanero/a	a plumber
un/a funcionario/a	a civil servant
un/a informático/a	a computer scientist
un/a ingeniero/a	an engineer
un/a médico/a	a doctor
un/a panadero/a	a baker
un/a periodista	a journalist
estar en paro	to be unemployed
el desempleo	unemployment

Using ser to say what jobs people do

Use the verb ser to say what jobs people do. Leave out the indefinite article:

Soy cocinero.   I'm a cook.
Es modelo.   She's a model.
Es camarero.   He's a waiter.

Feminine forms

If the job is done by a woman, change -o to -a and add -a to the ending -or:

cocinero ➡ cocinera   camarero ➡ camarera
agricultor ➡ agricultora

Note some exceptions: actor   actriz
Some jobs are the same in the masculine and feminine: periodista, dentista

trabajar in different tenses

Present	Imperfect	Future
trabajo	trabajaba	trabajaré
I work	I used to work	I will work

Worked example

Listen and answer the question in English. **(1 mark)**

How old is Paco? 30

Listen to the recording

– Hola. Me llamo Paco y tengo treinta años.

Listening strategies

✓ You'll hear every recording **twice**, so don't worry if you don't catch all the answers on first listening.
✓ Keep pace with the recording: if you've missed an answer, go on to the next question.
✓ Don't simply write down the first relevant item of vocabulary you hear. Make sure you listen to the **end** of a recording before you make your final decision.

Now try this

Listen to the recording

Listen to the rest of the recording from the worked example and answer the questions in English.

(a) Which job did Paco use to do? **(1 mark)**
(b) Why did Paco stop doing that job? **(1 mark)**
(c) What does he do now? **(1 mark)**
(d) What job will he do in the future? **(1 mark)**
(e) Why does he want to do this job? **(1 mark)**

Opinions about jobs

Be ready to understand and give a range of opinions on jobs – both positive and negative.

Opiniones sobre empleos

Me gusta tener responsabilidades.	I like having responsibility.
Me encanta trabajar en contacto con gente.	I love having contact with people.
Me gusta la variedad.	I like variety.
Me encanta trabajar en equipo.	I love working in a team.
Me gusta la flexibilidad.	I like flexibility.
Está bien pagado.	It's well paid.

Opiniones sobre empleos

Es un trabajo difícil.	It's a difficult job.
Odio trabajar solo.	I hate working alone.
No me gustan los clientes maleducados.	I don't like rude customers.
Está mal pagado.	It's badly paid.
Odio al jefe.	I hate the boss.
Trabajo muchas horas.	I work long hours.
Estoy de pie todo el día.	I'm on my feet all day.

Me gusta ayudar a la gente.
I like helping people.

Es aburrido y monótono.
It's boring and repetitive.

Worked example

Read the text.

> Trabajo en una comisaría y me encanta la responsabilidad que tengo. No gano mucho dinero porque el sueldo es bajo. Trabajo muchas horas, sobre todo el sábado y el domingo, pero trabajar los fines de semana me divierte más por la variedad de casos que hay.

Put a cross ✗ in the box beside the correct ending. **(1 mark)**

Gustavo works as a …

☐ **A** postal worker   ☐ **C** firefighter

☒ **B** police officer   ☐ **D** cashier

Exam alert

Make sure that you do not become distracted by the other options supplied in a multiple-choice question. Often you will find all the options in the text, but you must read carefully to work out the correct answer.

Knowing the places people work helps you make the link to their job:
una comisaría   a police station

It is important to learn little words like mucho (a lot) or poco (a little) as they can change the meaning quite radically. In this text, Gustavo says he does not earn much money, so you can rule out 'salary' as the answer to (a).

Now try this

Read the text in the worked example again and put a cross ✗ in the box beside the correct ending.

	A	B	C	D	
(a) Gustavo likes …	☐ the hours	☐ the salary	☐ the responsibility	☐ the boss	**(1 mark)**
(b) At the weekend, Gustavo's work is …	☐ boring	☐ exciting	☐ quiet	☐ varied	**(1 mark)**

Applying for jobs

Use this page to prepare for exam questions concerning job applications and interviews.

Solicitar trabajo

Un anuncio de oferta de trabajo	a job advert
Estimado/a señor/a	Dear Sir/Madam
Me dirijo a usted para solicitar el puesto de …	
I am writing to apply for the post of …	
Le adjunto mi currículum.	I attach my CV.
Domino perfectamente el alemán.	
I am a fluent German speaker.	
Tengo varias habilidades.	I have various skills.
He rellenado la solicitud.	
I have filled in the application form.	
Me he formado como aprendiz en …	
I have done an apprenticeship in …	
Quedo a su disposición.	I await your reply.
Le saluda atentamente	Yours sincerely / faithfully

Tenemos que pedir referencias. We have to ask for references.

Una entrevista de trabajo

¿Por qué quiere ser … ?	
Why do you want to be a … ?	
Quiero ser … porque …	
I want to be a … because …	
Me gustaría trabajar de …	
I would like to work as a …	
¿Cuál es su experiencia laboral?	
What work experience do you have?	
Tengo experiencia en …	I have experience in …
He trabajado como …	I have worked as a …
director / gerente	manager
representante de ventas	sales rep
He trabajado en mercadotecnia.	
I have worked in marketing.	
¿Qué cualidades personales tiene?	
What are your personal qualities?	
Soy creativo/a / ambicioso/a / trabajador/a.	
I am creative / ambitious / hardworking.	
¿Cuál es el horario de trabajo?	
What are the hours of work?	
De … a … / Desde … hasta …	From … until …

Worked example

LISTENING TRACK 37

Listen to the recording and answer the question **in English**.
What job interests Raúl? **(1 mark)**

cabin crew

Listen to the recording [QR code]

– Quiero ser auxiliar de vuelo porque me encanta trabajar con la gente.

What does Raúl want to be? That is what the question is asking. If you have forgotten that **auxiliar de vuelo** is 'cabin crew', you may remember that **vuelo** means 'flight', which should help you work out the answer.

Learning vocabulary

The more vocabulary you know, the easier you will find listening activities. When learning vocabulary, don't waste valuable time going over words you already know or can guess.

Use different techniques to help you learn more difficult vocabulary:
- ✓ Write out the word and then copy it out several times.
- ✓ Ask someone to test you.
- ✓ Say the word aloud many times and record yourself saying it.
- ✓ Make associations – draw a picture or think of a story to help you remember the word.

Now try this

LISTENING TRACK 38

Listen to the recording [QR code]

Listen to the whole recording from the worked example and put a cross ✗ by the **three** correct sentences. **(3 marks)**

☐ **A** Raúl never finds the customers difficult.
☐ **B** He is ambitious.
☐ **C** Belén wants to be a vet.
☐ **D** She has worked with sick people in America.
☐ **E** She has worked in a team.
☐ **F** She is not anti-social.

Had a look ☐ Nearly there ☐ Nailed it! ☐

Work experience

As well as the imperfect, you'll need to know the preterite tense to talk about work experience.

Experiencia laboral

¿Qué experiencia laboral tienes?	What work experience do you have?
Trabajaba en …	I was working in …
una oficina.	an office.
una tienda.	a shop.
un instituto.	a school.
Hacía fotocopias.	I made photocopies.
Trabajaba con niños.	I worked with children.
Llamaba por teléfono.	I made phone calls.
Ayudaba al jefe.	I helped the boss.
Utilizaba el ordenador.	I used the computer.
Ayudaba a los enfermos.	I helped sick people.

Vendía cosas a los clientes.
I sold things to customers.

Tenía que dar información a los clientes.
I had to give information to customers.

Mis colegas me ayudaron mucho.
My colleagues helped me a lot.

Aprendí un montón de cosas.
I learned a lot of things.

Imperfect or preterite?

✓ You use the **preterite** tense for a **single** event that took place in the past.
Empecé a trabajar a los dieciocho años.
I started working at 18.
Hice un curso de formación.
I did a training course.

✓ You use the **imperfect** tense for repeated or **continuous** actions in the past. In English we often translate them in the same way.
Archivaba documentos.
I filed (used to file) documents.
Siempre había quejas.
There were always complaints.

La jefa era bastante estricta.
The boss was quite strict.

Worked example

Listen to Fernando. Put a cross ✗ in the correct box. **(1 mark)**
Fernando talks about …
☐ **A** his colleagues   ☐ **C** the salary
☒ **B** his journey   ☐ **D** his hours

Listen to the recording

– Para llegar allí, primero tenía que coger el metro y después iba a pie.

Exam alert

Make sure that you read the instructions carefully and give exactly the number of answers required. In multiple-choice questions similar to this one, there will be four options (A, B, C, D) and you must only put a cross in **one** box.

Before the recording starts, think about the types of words you will be listening for, for each of the options:
A colegas, gente, etc.
B transporte, coche, etc.
C sueldo, dinero, etc.
D horas, horario, etc.

Now try this

Listen to the whole recording from the worked example and put a cross ✗ in each of the **three** correct boxes below. **(3 marks)**
Fernando talks about...
☐ **A** what he did at lunchtime
☐ **B** the disadvantages of his work
☐ **C** what he had to wear
☐ **D** what he had to do
☐ **E** the days he worked
☐ **F** the work he wants to do
☐ **G** the money he will earn

Listen to the recording

Key vocabulary to listen out for:
• work vocabulary (empleados, tenía que, etc.)
• phrases to introduce negative opinions (no me gusta, lo peor era, etc.)
• expressions relating to the future (cuando sea mayor).

Volunteering

Use this page to prepare for understanding texts about volunteering.

El voluntariado

Trabajé de / como voluntario/a ...	I worked voluntarily ...
Trabajamos sin cobrar ...	We worked without pay ...
Me ofrecí como voluntario ...	I became a volunteer ...
en una clínica.	in a clinic.
en un instituto.	in a school.
en una residencia de ancianos.	in an old people's home.
en zonas de conflicto.	in conflict zones.
al aire libre.	in the open air.

Hay muchas ventajas en este tipo de trabajo.
There are many advantages to this type of work.

Puedes aprender muchas habilidades nuevas.
You can learn lots of new skills.

Puedes adquirir experiencia en el área que te interese.
You can gain experience in the area you are interested in.

Es bueno ayudar a los más necesitados.
It is good to help those most in need.

Talking generally using 'you'

To talk generally about what someone **can** do, use the verb poder in the tú form in the present tense:

Puedes vivir una experiencia única.
You can experience something unique.

Or in the future tense:

Podrás trabajar con niños.
You will be able to work with children.

Or use it in the él/ella form with the impersonal pronoun se:

Se puede conocer a todo tipo de personas.
You can get to know all types of people.

Use the verb deber to say what someone **should** do. You can use the present tense with the tú form:

Debes dedicar tu tiempo a los démas.
You should dedicate your time to others.

Or, to sound more formal, use the conditional tense of deber in the él/ella form with pronoun se:

Se debería ofrecer tiempo para ayudar a los demás.
You should offer time to help others.

Worked example

Listen to Juan. Put a cross ✗ in the **two** correct boxes. **(2 marks)**

Volunteering ...

☐ **A** is hard work   ☐ **D** is now more popular
☒ **B** makes you feel good   ☐ **E** is not for everyone
☒ **C** can teach you work skills

– El voluntariado es bueno para los demás, pero también para uno mismo. Aunque no esté remunerado, puedes realizar tareas que tengan relación con tu carrera profesional o puesto de trabajo; esto te ayudará a ganar experiencia para futuros trabajos.

Listen to the recording

The vocabulary surrounding this topic is quite difficult. However, use your deductive skills to pick out key words and phrases in order to answer successfully: para uno mismo (for oneself), ganar experiencia (to gain experience) para futuros trabajos (for future jobs).

Now try this

Listen to the recording

Listen to the whole recording from the worked example and answer the questions **in English**.

(a) What will volunteering help you with? **(1 mark)**

(b) When did Juan volunteer? **(1 mark)**

(c) What did Juan gain from the experience? **(1 mark)**

(d) What is his opinion about his own voluntary work? **(1 mark)**

Helping others

Be prepared to talk about how you help other people or how you would like to help.

Ayudar a otros

¿Por qué se debería ayudar a otros?
Why should you help other people?

Es bueno ser generoso y simpático.
It's good to be generous and kind.

Si haces cosas buenas por los demás te sentirás mejor contigo mismo.
If you do good deeds for other people you will feel better about yourself.

Para ayudar a mis padres trato de …
To help my parents I try to …

limpiar la casa.	clean the house.
poner la mesa.	lay the table.
quitar la mesa.	clear the table.
planchar la ropa.	iron clothes.
fregar los platos.	do the washing up.
pasar la aspiradora.	do the vacuuming.
arreglar mi habitación.	tidy my room.

The imperfect tense
Grammar page 94

Remember to use the imperfect when you describe what you used to do, as well as the following time phrases:

antes	before
a menudo	often
siempre	always
nunca	never
todos los días / cada día	every day

Antes no ayudaba mucho a mis padres pero ahora paso la aspiradora cada semana.
I did not use to help my parents very much but now I do the vacuuming every week.

Worked example

Lee el artículo.

¿Ayudas a los demás?

Es importante ayudar a tu familia a menudo; ofrecer ayuda con las tareas domésticas o con tareas de cualquier otro tipo. Ayudar es especialmente importante cuando ves que algún miembro de tu familia o de tus amigos parece estresado o está muy ocupado, son estas personas las que realmente van a apreciar tu ayuda.

¿Qué tipos de tareas puedes hacer por ellos? Pues una de las más fáciles, y de las más agradecidas, es preparar una comida para ellos o ir al supermercado. Hacer la compra y cocinar para los demás es un acto generoso y especialmente útil si alguien, aunque no esté ocupado, no se encuentra bien.

¿Y ayudar a hermanos o primos más pequeños? Ofrece hacer de canguro y así das un descanso bien merecido a sus padres. Tu ayuda será recompensada con gran agradecimiento y reconocimiento. ¡Te sentirás genial!

Contesta la pregunta **en español**.
¿Cuándo es bueno ofrecer ayuda a un amigo?
(1 mark)

Cuando parece estresado / cuando está muy ocupado

To help you find the answer, you need to read the first two sentences carefully. The text states that you should help your family often (**es importante ayudar a tu familia a menudo**) but mentions helping friends when they are stressed or busy (**cuando ves que algún miembro de tu familia o de tus amigos parece estresado o está muy ocupado**).

Now try this

Lee el artículo otra vez y contesta las preguntas **en español**.
(a) ¿Qué puedes hacer para ayudar a alguien que no se siente bien? **(1 mark)**
(b) ¿Cómo puedes ayudar a los familiares con niños? **(1 mark)**

Charities

Be prepared for understanding texts about charitable causes and fundraising.

La caridad

una fundación benéfica	a charitable foundation
una campaña global	a worldwide campaign
una organización benéfica	a charitable organisation
Es a / en beneficio de ...	It's in aid of ...
recaudar fondos	to fundraise
organizar una venta benéfica	to organise a charity sale
asistir a una venta de pasteles	to attend a cake sale
participar en una carrera	to take part in a race

publicar los eventos benéficos en las redes sociales
to publicise charity events on social media

Doy dinero porque ...	I give money because ...
me importa.	it matters to me.
puedo marcar la diferencia.	I can make a difference.
quiero ayudar a los demás.	I want to help others.

me gustaría mejorar la vida de los demás.
I would like to make other people's lives better.

Using Ojalá to say 'Let's hope!'
Grammar page 99

Ojalá is a word which means 'let's hope' or 'if only'. You need to use the subjunctive after this word.
Ojalá la situación mejore.
Let's hope the situation improves.
Ojalá pudiera correr un maratón.
If only I could run a marathon.

Use expressions like these in your writing and speaking if you want to aim for a high grade.

Worked example

Lee el artículo.
Completa cada frase con una palabra del recuadro de abajo.

niños   personas   pobres   países
colegios   campañas   enfermos

La organización trabaja en muchos
..países.. **(1 mark)**

When completing the gaps in an exercise, make sure your answer not only makes sense, but also is grammatically correct. For example, in question (b) you are looking for an adjective, not a noun.

Save the Children

Trabajamos para que millones de niños tengan la oportunidad de ser lo que quieren ser hoy, de soñar lo que serán mañana y de construir un mundo mejor. Llegamos a 55 millones de niños gracias a las 25.000 personas que trabajamos en más de 120 países. Actualmente uno de cada tres niños en España está en riesgo de pobreza o exclusión social. La infancia de nuestro país es el colectivo que más está sufriendo las consecuencias del desempleo y de los recortes en las ayudas sociales. Por ello, centramos nuestro trabajo en España en luchar contra la pobreza infantil. La educación es la herramienta más poderosa para romper el ciclo de transmisión de la pobreza de padres a hijos.

Now try this

Lee el artículo de nuevo. Completa cada frase con una palabra del recuadro de arriba. No necesitas todas las palabras.

(a) Veinticinco mil es el número de .... que trabajan en el mundo para la organización. **(1 mark)**

(b) Ahora hay más niños españoles .... debido a la crisis económica. **(1 mark)**

(c) Trabajan en .... para cambiar la situación en España. **(1 mark)**

Careers and training

Be prepared to talk about professions that you are interested in.

Las profesiones y la formación

Tengo mucha ambición.
I have lots of ambition.

Quiero tener la licenciatura en …
I want to have a degree in …

Tengo la idea de hacer un internado.
I am thinking of doing an internship.

Estoy pensando en hacer prácticas.
I am thinking about doing work experience.

Tengo que elegir la carrera adecuada.
I have to choose a suitable career.

(No) se necesita el bachillerato para ser …
You (don't) need A-levels to be …

Hay que realizar un curso de formación.
You have to do a training course.

Word families

Learning groups of words together and making mind maps is a great way of learning more vocabulary and preparing yourself for more difficult texts. When you learn a new noun, verb or adjective, see if there are any other related words.

médico   doctor ➡ medicina   medicine

estudiar   to study ➡
el estudiante   student ➡
los estudios   studies

Worked example

Mira la foto y prepara tus respuestas a los puntos siguientes:
- la descripción de la foto
- la profesión que más te interesa
- tu opinión de trabajar como voluntario
- tu experiencia del trabajo en el pasado
- la importancia de encontrar un trabajo bien pagado.

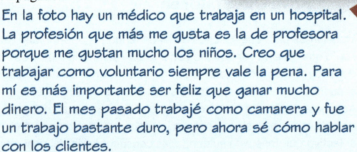

En la foto hay un médico que trabaja en un hospital. La profesión que más me gusta es la de profesora porque me gustan mucho los niños. Creo que trabajar como voluntario siempre vale la pena. Para mí es más importante ser feliz que ganar mucho dinero. El mes pasado trabajé como camarera y fue un trabajo bastante duro, pero ahora sé cómo hablar con los clientes.

Aiming Higher

En la foto se ve un médico que trabaja en un hospital. Ser médico no es una profesión que me interesa porque no quiero seguir estudiando ciencias. El año pasado trabajé como voluntario en una iglesia y aprendí muchas cosas que me ayudarán a lo largo de mi carrera. En verano trabajé de recepcionista en un camping y lo mejor fue que aprendí a atender a clientes descontentos. Me gustaría ser licenciada en Arquitectura. Haría prácticas en una empresa internacional y aprendería a diseñar. La Arquitectura es una profesión muy variada y también bien pagada, pero esto no es lo más importante para mí.

Exam alert

Think about the tenses to use for each bullet point and also how you can justify any opinions you give. The examiner may prompt you by asking ¿Por qué? or ¿Algo más?

It's important to justify your opinions: – porque me gustan mucho los niños; para mí es más importante ser feliz.

A good range of verbs in the conditional tense (me gustaría) and the impersonal se (se ve un médico) help to make this answer more complex. Using the irregular verb hacer in the conditional (haría prácticas) also shows good verb knowledge.

Now try this

Answer the following questions:
- ¿Qué profesión te gustaría hacer?
- ¿Es importante encontrar un trabajo bien pagado?

Messages

Learn this language to help you understand different types of messages.

Mensajes

¿Sí? / Dígame.	Hello? (when answering the phone)
el prefijo	area code
Llámame / Llámeme.	Call me (informal / formal).
Te llamaré / Le llamaré.	I'll call you (back) (informal / formal).
Espera.	Wait.
No cuelgue.	Stay on the line.
Te paso / Le paso.	I will put you through (informal / formal).
en la línea	on the line
de momento	at the moment
por teléfono	by phone
el contestador	voicemail
el auricular	the (telephone) receiver
marcar el número	dial the number

número equivocado	wrong number
Vuelvo enseguida.	I'll be right back.
Deje un mensaje.	Leave a message.
a la atención de …	for the attention of …
después de la señal	after the tone
mi número de móvil	my mobile number

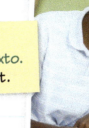

Envíame un mensaje de texto. Send me a text.

Worked example

Listen to the recording

Listen and answer the question **in English**.
Why has the caller got Jesús's answering machine?

(1 mark)

He's on holiday.

– ¡Hola! Ha llamado al contestador automático de Jesús. Ahora no estoy aquí porque estoy de vacaciones …

- Spanish telephone numbers consist of nine numbers, often starting 9 or 8 for landlines and 6 for mobiles. They are normally written as follows: 657 87 42 19
This is usually said as: **seis, cinco, siete; ochenta y siete; cuarenta y dos; diecinueve**
- Remember: you have **five minutes** to look at the questions. You are obviously going to hear several numbers, so make sure you are prepared for that.

Now try this

Listen to the whole recording from the worked example and answer these questions **in English**.

(a) What other contact number does Jesús give? **(1 mark)**
(b) The second answering machine is for which company? **(1 mark)**
(c) What are the opening times of the company? **(1 mark)**
(d) What alternative number does the company give? **(1 mark)**

Listen to the recording

Part-time jobs

When talking about a part-time job, use tener que to discuss your responsibilities.

Empleos a tiempo parcial

los fines de semana	at weekends
después del instituto	after school
Trabajo para / en ...	I work for / in ...
un empresario	an employer
un diseñador	a designer
un electricista	an electrician
un negocio	a business
una sastrería	a tailor's
una agencia de viajes	a travel agency
Estoy muy ocupado/a.	I am very busy.

Escucho el contestador automático.
I listen to the answering machine.

Leo mensajes.	I read messages.
Me pagan por hora.	They pay me by the hour.

Las condiciones de trabajo son buenas.
The working conditions are good.

Está bien / mal pagado. It is well / badly paid.

Prepositions

Prepositions come up in every topic: they give information about **where**, **when** and **how** things happen.

a	to / at	para	for / in
con	with		order to
de	from	por	for / by
desde	from, since	sin	without
en	in, on	sobre	on, about
entre	between		

en nuestra página web	on our web page
por fax	by fax
para conseguir más información	in order to know more information
sin experiencia	without experience

Trabajo en la biblioteca de la universidad.
I work in the university library.

Worked example

Read the advert.

> **OFERTAS DE EMPLEO**
> Multimundo – Se necesita secretario sin experiencia para trabajar a tiempo parcial en una empresa multinacional. Los interesados tienen que rellenar un formulario en nuestra página web. Ofrecemos formación, buen sueldo y buen horario. Las entrevistas tendrán lugar dentro de un mes.

Put a cross ✗ in the box beside the correct ending.
(1 mark)

The job ...
- ☒ **A** is not full time
- ☐ **B** is for a small company
- ☐ **C** does not offer any training
- ☐ **D** will not require an interview

Reading strategies

✓ Answers to questions are usually found in the text in the **order** in which they are asked – so you won't usually find the first answer right at the end.

✓ You need to read carefully to pick up the **detail**. Reading to get the gist alone will not give you all the information you need.

Read the statements carefully and think about whether they are positive or negative. 'Not full time' obviously means it is part-time, so the answer is A, as the text states trabajar a tiempo parcial.

Now try this

Read the text in the worked example again and put a cross ✗ in the box beside the **three** correct sentences. **(3 marks)**

- ☐ **A** Secretarial experience is required.
- ☐ **B** The company has branches in different countries.
- ☐ **C** Applications must be made by post.
- ☐ **D** There is more information on the web page.
- ☐ **E** The salary is good.
- ☐ **F** The hours of work are long.
- ☐ **G** The interviews will take place in a month's time.

Money

Topics concerning money always involve numbers. Make sure you know them.

El dinero

Tengo un trabajo a tiempo parcial.
I have a part-time job.

Recibo una paga semanal de mis padres.
I receive weekly pocket money from my parents.

Ahorro dinero.   I save money.

Lo pongo en una caja en mi habitación.
I put it in a box in my room.

Recargo el saldo del móvil cada quince días.
I buy credit for my mobile every fortnight.

Me lo gasto en …   I spend it on …

revistas   caramelos   ropa

maquillaje   pendientes   libros / novelas

Direct object pronouns

Grammar page 87

Use direct object pronouns to avoid repeating a noun.

¿Te gustan los caramelos?
  Sí, los compro cada quince días.
Do you like sweets?
  Yes, I buy them every fortnight.

Recibo dinero de mis padres.
  Lo ahorro para descargar música.
I get money from my parents.
  I save it to download music.

The pronoun agrees in number and gender with the noun it replaces:

	Singular	Plural
Masculine	el dinero ➡ lo	los libros ➡ los
Feminine	la ropa ➡ la	las novelas ➡ las

Worked example

LISTENING TRACK 45

Listen and answer the question **in English**.   **(2 marks)**
What does she not spend her pocket money on?
Make-up or concert tickets

Listen to the recording

> Mis hermanas se lo gastan en maquillaje o entradas para conciertos pero yo no.

Remember to listen out carefully for negatives. It's when she talks about her sisters that she tells us what she does **not** buy.

Exam alert

The listening extract for each numbered question will be played **twice** without any pauses. After the second play, there will be a **pause** to give you time to complete your answers before you need to listen to the next numbered question.

Remember: if a question is divided into several questions or tasks labelled with letters (a), (b), etc., this means they all relate to the same extract. So make sure you listen for all these answers in one go so that you don't miss out.

In question (a), the verb forms to listen out for are conditional or future, as she will talk about her future plans.

Now try this

LISTENING TRACK 46

Listen to the whole recording from the worked example and answer the questions **in English**.

(a) Why is she saving her money?   **(1 mark)**
(b) What did she use to do with her money?   **(2 marks)**
(c) Why won't she get pocket money from her parents next year?   **(1 mark)**

Listen to the recording

Sporting events

You will need to understand and use language related to sporting events.

Los eventos deportivos

Las ventajas son ...   The advantages are ...
Hay un ambiente especial.
There is a special atmosphere.
El evento que más me interesa es ...
The event that most interests me is ...
Creo que los eventos están bien porque ...
I think the events are good because ...
 promueven el turismo.
 they encourage tourism.
 regeneran las zonas urbanas.
 they regenerate urban areas.
 fomentan la participación en el deporte.
 they promote participation in sport.
 inspiran a los jóvenes.
 they inspire young people.
 crean oportunidades de empleo.
 they create job opportunities.

Las desventajas son ... The disadvantages are ...
Las medidas de seguridad
 cuestan mucho.
The security measures cost a lot.
No soy fan de los acontecimientos
 deportivos internacionales.
I am not a fan of international events.
Siempre hay grandes colas para entrar al evento.
There are always big queues to enter the event.
La gente se preocupa por ...
People worry about ...
Generan mucho tráfico.
They create lots of traffic.
Los costes de organización son altos.
They cost a lot to organise.

Worked example

Escribe un artículo sobre los deportes. **Debes** incluir los puntos siguientes: **(15 marks)**
- por qué los grandes eventos deportivos son importantes
- la última vez que asististe a un evento deportivo.

> Los eventos deportivos están bien porque inspiran a los jóvenes. El problema es que cuestan mucho. Hace unos años fui a los Juegos Olímpicos en mi ciudad y vi unas carreras de natación. Fue una experiencia inolvidable.

Aiming Higher

> A mi modo de ver, los grandes eventos deportivos son excelentes porque fomentan la participación en el deporte y crean bastantes oportunidades de empleo. Además, hacen crecer la economía y unen a la gente.
> Uno de los inconvenientes es que las medidas de seguridad cuestan mucho. El año pasado, mi familia y yo fuimos a un partido de la Copa del Mundo de rugby que tuvo lugar en mi país. La "haka" del equipo de Nueva Zelanda fue increíble.

Writing strategies

You will be asked to give your opinion in the writing exam, and the bullet points could do this in various ways:
- ☑ ¿Por qué vale la pena ... ?
- ☑ ¿Por qué ... son importantes / populares?
- ☑ Lo que piensas de ...
- ☑ Lo más interesante de ...

Make sure you recognise that these prompts are asking for an opinion, and remember to justify the opinion by giving reasons.

Interesting opinion phrases such as **a mi modo de ver** and a variety of connectives such as **además** make this candidate's language more sophisticated. Giving the other side of the argument, with **uno de los inconvenientes es**, also shows competence in expressing ideas.

Now try this

Write your own article, including the information requested in the bullet points in the worked example.
Write at least 60–70 words. **(15 marks)**

Music events

Be prepared to talk about concerts and music events.

Los eventos musicales

Mis amigos y yo fuimos a un concierto.
My friends and I went to a concert.
Estuve tres horas en el concierto.
I spent three hours at the concert.
Bailamos mucho.   We danced a lot.
El grupo cantó todas mis canciones preferidas.
The band sang all my favourite songs.
Mi amigo me compró una camiseta.
My friend bought me a T-shirt.
Saqué muchas fotos.   I took lots of photos.
Mis amigos comieron hamburguesas y bebieron limonada.
My friends ate burgers and drank lemonade.
El espectáculo fue impresionante.
The show was impressive.
Lo pasamos bomba.   We had a great time.
El escenario era muy grande. The stage was really big.
Había más de 20.000 espectadores.
There were more than 20,000 spectators.
El ambiente estaba animado.   The atmosphere was lively.

Expressing opinions about past events

Use the **preterite** tense to give your opinion about an event that has already taken place.

El concierto fue estupendo.
The concert was great.
Me divertí mucho.
I enjoyed myself a lot.
Lo pasé muy bien.
I had a really good time.
Me gustó escuchar mis canciones favoritas.
I liked listening to my favourite songs.
Fuimos a un concierto de rock y fue sensacional.
We went to a rock concert and it was sensational.

Worked example

SPEAKING

Mira la foto y prepara tus respuestas a los siguientes puntos:

- la descripción de la foto
- lo que piensas de los eventos musicales
- un concierto que te ha gustado
- tu preferencia: ver un evento musical o deportivo
- un evento musical o deportivo al que te gustaría asistir.

Háblame de la foto.
En esta foto la gente está en un estadio escuchando un concierto de música rock. Hay muchos espectadores y el escenario es bastante grande.
A mí me gustan los eventos musicales. ¿Y a ti?
En realidad me encantan los eventos musicales porque cuando hay mucha gente el ambiente es increíble.
Háblame de un concierto al que has asistido o que has visto, por ejemplo, en la televisión.
Mis amigos y yo fuimos a un concierto de nuestro grupo favorito. Bailamos mucho porque conocíamos todas las canciones. Fue una experiencia muy emocionante.
¿Prefieres los eventos musicales o los eventos deportivos?
Por lo general prefiero los eventos musicales. A mi modo de ver, son más divertidos porque el público participa más.
Me gustaría ir a un concierto de rock con mi novio.

Exam alert

In your speaking tasks:
- Respond to each question as fully as you can.
- If you need to hear a question again, you can ask the examiner to repeat it.
- Do use the preparation time to think about your answers, but don't read out whole sentences that you've prepared in advance.

Now try this

Give your own answers to the questions in the worked example.

Green issues

Make sure you know vocabulary relating to the environment.

Los problemas medioambientales

Los problemas más graves son ...
The most serious problems are ...

la contaminación / la polución — pollution

la destrucción de la capa de ozono
the destruction of the ozone layer

el cambio climático — climate change

el calentamiento global — global warming

las inundaciones — floods

la destrucción de la selva tropical
the destruction of the rainforest

el aumento de las sequías
the increase in droughts

las especies en peligro de extinción
species in danger of extinction

la falta de recursos naturales
the lack of natural resources

la contaminación de los océanos
pollution of the oceans

la basura — rubbish

el planeta — the planet

los terremotos — earthquakes

Phrases with the subjunctive

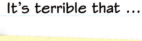
Grammar page 99

Learn some expressions that use the subjunctive to improve your speaking and show you can use complex structures. Use the present subjunctive after these expressions:

Es importante que ... — It's important that ...
Es esencial que ... — It's essential that ...
Es increíble que ... — It's incredible that ...
Es terrible que ... — It's terrible that ...

Es importante que separemos la basura.
It's important that we sort our rubbish.

Worked example

• ¿Cuáles son los problemas más graves del planeta?

Para mí, el problema más grande es el calentamiento global. Pienso que deberíamos usar más el transporte público y reutilizar más productos.

Aiming Higher

Es esencial que trabajemos contra la destrucción de la capa de ozono si queremos salvar nuestro planeta. Es necesario que reciclemos más y no deberíamos malgastar electricidad ni consumir tanta energía. Además, compraré pilas recargables y nunca más utilizaré bolsas de plástico.

Speaking strategies

Try not to use English sounds when you hesitate, such as 'um' or 'er'. Instead, fill any gaps with Spanish equivalents – pues, a ver, es decir.

This is a satisfactory answer but it could be improved.

Here various tenses are used effectively, as well as the subjunctive:
Es esencial que trabajemos ... ,
Es necesario que reciclemos ...
The use of connectives and conjunctions such as si and además also helps raise the level.

Now try this

• ¿Cuáles son los problemas más graves del planeta?

Environmental action

Learn how to use 'if' clauses so you can use them in the writing exam.

Proteger el medioambiente

Se debe ...	You should ...
No se debe ...	You should not ...
evitar	avoid
correr el riesgo de	run the risk of
aumentar	increase
reducir	reduce
malgastar	waste
dedicarse a	devote time to
intentar a	try to
lograr	achieve
ocuparse de	to be concerned with
ponerse a	start
quejarse de	complain about
usar el transporte público	use public transport
apagar las luces	turn off lights
proteger la naturaleza	protect nature
separar la basura	recyle your rubbish
usar bolsas de plástico	use plastic bags
en vez de	instead of

'If' clauses

In clauses with si (if), you need to use the correct verb forms:

✓ Si + present tense + future tense

Si no malgastamos la energía, será mejor para el medio ambiente.
If we don't waste electricity, it will be better for the environment.

✓ Si + imperfect subjunctive + conditional

Si todo el mundo se dedicara a no utilizar las bolsas plásticas, no habría tanto residuo tóxico.
If everyone tried not to use plastic bags, there would not be as much toxic waste.

Worked example

Escribe un texto sobre el medioambiente. **Debes** incluir el punto siguiente:

• lo que haces para proteger el medioambiente.

Quiero proteger el planeta y por eso siempre separo la basura. Reciclo el vidrio, el papel y el plástico y siempre uso los contenedores correctos.

Aiming Higher

Sin duda me ocupo mucho del medioambiente. Mi familia siempre compra productos ecológicos, ya que no contienen productos químicos malos. He comprado un bonobús, así que puedo usar el transporte público a menudo y es barato. Claro que es mejor que viajar en coche todo el tiempo. Si más gente fuese a pie o en autobús, reduciríamos la contaminación del aire.

This piece of writing has a good range of verb forms:
• compra, contienen ➡ present
• he comprado ➡ perfect
• fuese ➡ imperfect subjunctive
• reduciríamos ➡ conditional
It also contains some interesting conjunctions, ya que and así que, as well as connectives such as claro que and sin duda.

Now try this

Escribe un texto de 130–150 palabras sobre el medioambiente. **Debes** incluir los puntos siguientes: **(28 marks)**

• por qué es importante proteger el medioambiente
• tu opinión sobre las bolsas de plástico
• lo que has hecho recientemente
• lo que vas a hacer en el futuro.

Global issues

Use this page to learn how to talk about important issues affecting the world.

Los problemas globales

los desastres naturales	natural disasters
la falta de agua potable	lack of drinking water
el hambre mundial	world hunger
la guerra	war
los derechos humanos	human rights
los necesitados	the disadvantaged
la pobreza	poverty
la crisis económica	the economic crisis
el crimen en Internet	internet crime

las personas sin hogar
homeless people

Key verbs for expressing ideas

Use these key verbs to help you discuss serious global issues.

compartir	to share
darse cuenta de	to realise
enseñar	to teach
investigar	to research
mostrar	to show
notar	to note
parar	to stop
tratar de	to try to

En mi opinión, tenemos que tratar de parar el hambre mundial.

In my opinion we have to try to end world hunger.

Worked example

Read this extract from *Los Valores y Sus Desafíos Actuales* by José Ramón Fabelo Corzo.

> Los problemas globales son aquellos que afectan los intereses de toda la comunidad mundial, que amenazan el futuro de la humanidad, que atentan contra las posibilidades de desarrollo de la civilización. Entre los problemas globales que tradicionalmente se incluyen en diferentes listados se encuentran los siguientes: la gran desproporción en los niveles de desarrollo social y económico entre las distintas partes del planeta, las amenazas a la seguridad y la paz internacional, la problemática ecológica, y el agotamiento de los recursos naturales no renovables.

Put a cross ✗ in the box beside the correct ending.   **(1 mark)**

Global issues are ...

☐ **A** always environmental
☐ **B** increasing substantially
☒ **C** a danger to our existence
☐ **D** not of interest to everyone

Unfamiliar words

✓ In texts such as these, there may be words you have never seen before. Revise vocabulary carefully to give yourself the best preparation. Then use strategies to work out unfamiliar words.

✓ Sometimes Spanish words add an -o or an -a to the end of a word ending in a consonant in English.

✓ Often words that end in -dad in Spanish end in '-ity' in English:
la comunidad – community
la humanidad – humanity

✓ Spanish words ending in -ión are almost always cognates or near-cognates:
la civilización – civilization
la desproporción – disproportion

Now try this

Read the text in the worked example again and put a cross ✗ in the correct box.   **(1 mark)**

Global problems mentioned include . . .

☐ **A** threats to our security and green issues
☐ **B** poverty and crime
☐ **C** consumerism and green issues
☐ **D** violence and lack of drinking water

Natural resources

Make sure you learn a range of vocabulary about looking after the planet.

Los recursos naturales

cuidar la tierra — to look after the earth
proteger el campo — to protect the countryside
convertir en abono — to compost
evitar el malgasto de … — to prevent wasting …
consumir — to consume
el consumo — consumption
reciclar — to recycle
el reciclaje — recycling
reutilizar — to reuse
ahorrar — to save, economise
la electricidad — electricity
el carbón — coal
la energía — energy
la energía solar — solar power
el gas — gas
el petróleo — oil
el agua dulce — fresh water
el agua salada — salt water
la pesca — fishing

The perfect tense

Grammar page 97

At Foundation level, you need to know the most common verbs in the perfect tense.

He usado el transporte público en Londres.
I have used public transport in London.

At Higher level, you need to know how to use the perfect tense of a wider range of verbs, including irregular verbs.

He puesto el vidrio en el contenedor de reciclaje.
I have put the glass in the recycling container.

Ahorro energía / electricidad.
I save electricity.

Worked example

Lee el texto.
Contesta la pregunta en **español**.
¿Cuál es el mensaje de la campaña 'Reflexiones'?
(1 mark)

Aunque no sea tu basura, sí es tu problema.

El Proyecto Libera lanza la campaña 'Reflexiones', una nueva acción con la que pretende concienciar a la ciudadanía sobre la importancia de mantener limpio nuestro entorno a través del mensaje 'aunque no sea tu basura, sí es tu problema'. Para ello, ha difundido tres vídeos en los que se muestra el ecosistema terrestre, fluvial y marino, con datos sobre el impacto que tiene el abandono de residuos en estos entornos para el medio ambiente.

Con esta campaña, queremos poner de manifiesto que todos somos parte de la solución. Entre todos podemos ayudar a mantener nuestro planeta, simplemente realizando pequeñas acciones diarias que no suponen un esfuerzo para nosotros, como guardar los residuos para tirarlos después en el contenedor adecuado y que, sin embargo, generan un gran beneficio para el planeta.

Now try this

Contesta las preguntas en español.

(a) ¿Sobre qué tres entornos tratan los vídeos? **(1 mark)**

(b) ¿Qué quieren demostrar con la campaña? **(1 mark)**

(c) ¿Qué podemos hacer a diario para ayudar? **(1 mark)**

Nouns and articles

Here you'll find out about the gender of nouns and how to use the correct article.

Gender

Nouns are words that name things and people. Every Spanish noun has a gender – masculine (m) or feminine (f). If a word ends in -o or -a, it's easy to work out the gender.

ends in -o	masculine – el bolso
ends in -a	feminine – la pera

Exceptions:

el día	day	la foto	photo
el turista	tourist	la moto	motorbike
el problema	problem	la mano	hand

For words ending in any other letter, you need to learn the word with the article. If you don't know the gender, look it up in a dictionary.

cine nm cinema

noun masculine – so el cine

The definite article

The definite article ('the') changes to match the gender and number of the noun.

	Singular	Plural
Masculine	el libro	los libros
Feminine	la casa	las casas

The definite article is sometimes used in Spanish when we don't use it in English:

✓ with abstract nouns (things you can't see / touch)

El turismo es importante.	Tourism is important.

✓ with likes and dislikes

Me gusta el francés.	I like French.

✓ with days of the week to say 'on'

el domingo	on Sunday
los domingos	on Sundays

No me gustan nada las ciencias.
I don't like science at all.

The indefinite article

The indefinite article ('a / an') changes to match the gender and number of the noun. In the plural, the English is 'some' or 'any'.

	Singular	Plural
Masculine	un libro	unos libros
Feminine	una casa	unas casas

The indefinite article is NOT used when you talk about jobs.

Soy profesor. I'm a teacher.

Plurals

Plurals are easy to form in Spanish.

Singular	Plural
ends in a vowel un tomate	add -s unos tomates
ends in any consonant except -z la región	add -es las regiones
ends in -z el pez	drop z and add -ces los peces

Now try this

1 Make these nouns plural.

(a) folleto ....

(b) vez ....

(c) tradición ....

(d) café ....

(e) actor ....

2 El or la? Use a dictionary to fill in the articles.

(a) .... ciudad

(b) .... pijama

(c) .... pintor

(d) .... educación

(e) .... imagen

Adjectives

When using adjectives, you have to think about **agreement** and **position**.

Adjective agreement

Adjectives describe nouns. They must agree with the noun in gender (masculine or feminine) and number (singular or plural).

Adjective	Singular	Plural
ending in -o		
Masculine	alto	altos
Feminine	alta	altas
ending in -e		
Masculine	inteligente	inteligentes
Feminine	inteligente	inteligentes
ending in a consonant		
Masculine	azul	azules
Feminine	azul	azules

A dictionary shows the masculine form of an adjective. Make sure you don't forget to make it agree when it's feminine and / or plural!
las faldas amarillas   the yellow skirts

Note the exceptions:

ending in -or		
Masculine	hablador	habladores
Feminine	habladora	habladoras
adjectives of nationality ending in -s		
Masculine	inglés	ingleses
Feminine	inglesa	inglesas

Position of adjectives

Most Spanish adjectives come **after** the noun.
una falda azul   a blue skirt
These adjectives always come **before** the noun:

mucho	a lot	próximo	next
poco	a little	último	last
primero	first	alguno	some / any
segundo	second	ninguno	no
tercero	third		

Tengo muchos amigos. I have a lot of friends.

grande comes **before** the noun when it means 'great' rather than 'big'. It changes to gran before both masculine and feminine singular nouns.
Fue una gran película. It was a great film.

Short forms of adjectives

Some adjectives are shortened when they come before a masculine singular noun.

bueno	good	buen
malo	bad	mal
primero	first	primer
alguno	some / any	algún
ninguno	no	ningún

Pablo es un buen amigo.
Pablo is a good friend.

Now try this

Complete the text. (Look at the adjective endings to work out where they go.) Then translate the text into English.

bonitas   ruidosos   interesantes   internacionales   pequeña   habladora   históricos   simpática

Mallorca es una isla .... Tiene muchas playas .... En Mallorca hay muchos turistas
.... La gente allí es muy .... y es muy .... Mallorca tiene muchos museos
.... y muchos bares .... Se puede hacer muchas cosas ....

Possessives and pronouns

Use possessives to talk about who things belong to. Using pronouns will also help you sound more fluent.

Possessive adjectives

Possessive adjectives agree with the noun they describe, **not** the owner, e.g. sus botas – his boots.

	Singular	Plural
my	mi	mis
your	tu	tus
his / her / its	su	sus
our	nuestro / a	nuestros / as
your	vuestro / a	vuestros / as
their	su	sus

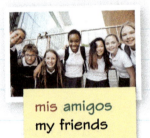

mis amigos
my friends

su colegio
their school

Possessive pronouns

These agree with the noun they replace, e.g. Su chaqueta es más elegante que la mía. His jacket is smarter than mine.

	Singular	
mine	el mío	la mía
yours	el tuyo	la tuya
his / hers / its	el suyo	la suya
ours	el nuestro	la nuestra
yours	el vuestro	la vuestra
theirs	el suyo	la suya

	Plural	
mine	los míos	las mías
yours	los tuyos	las tuyas
his / hers / its	los suyos	las suyas
ours	los nuestros	las nuestras
yours	los vuestros	las vuestras
theirs	los suyos	las suyas

Prepositional pronouns

These are used after prepositions.

para – for	mí – me	nosotros / as – us
por – for	ti – you	vosotros / as – you
sin – without	él – him	ellos – them (m)
a – to	ella – her	ellas – them (f)

Esta chaqueta es para ti.
This jacket is for you.

Note the accent on mí.

con + mí ➡ conmigo   with me
con + ti ➡ contigo   with you

The relative pronoun que

que ('which', 'that' or 'who') allows you to refer back to someone or something already mentioned. You must include it in Spanish, even when you might omit it in English.

El profesor que enseña francés.
The teacher who teaches French.
El libro que lee es español.
The book (that / which) he is reading is Spanish.

Now try this

Circle the correct form each time. Then translate the text into English.

Mis / Mi padrastro se llama Omar. **Su / Sus** hijas son mis hermanastras. **Mi / Mis** hermanastra, **que / por** se llama Sara, tiene un novio, Amit. **Su / Sus** novio es mayor que **el mío / la mía**. Salgo con **él / ella** desde hace seis años. Sara sale con **el suyo / las suyas** desde hace un mes.

Comparisons

If you're aiming for a higher grade, use structures like the comparative and superlative.

The comparative

The comparative is used to compare two things. It is formed as follows:

> más + adjective + que = more ... than
> menos + adjective + que = less ... than
> tan + adjective + como = as ... as

The adjective agrees with the noun it describes.

La música es más interesante que el deporte.
Music is more interesting than sport.

Pablo es menos alto que su hermano.
Pablo is shorter (less tall) than his brother.

Mi habitación es tan pequeña como la tuya.
My bedroom is as small as yours.

The superlative

The superlative is used to compare more than two things. It is formed as follows:

> el / la / los / las (+ noun) + más + adjective = the most ...
> el / la / los / las (+ noun) + menos + adjective = the least ...

The definite article and the adjective agree with the noun described.

Sydney es la ciudad más grande de Australia.
Sydney is the biggest city in Australia.

Esta casa es la menos cara del pueblo.
This house is the least expensive in the village.

Irregulars

Learn these useful irregular forms:

Adjective	Comparative	Superlative
good	better	the best
bueno	mejor	el / la mejor los / las mejores
bad	worse	the worst
malo	peor	el / la peor los / las peores

Este hotel es el mejor de la región.
This hotel is the best in the region.

Los restaurantes de aquí son los peores.
The restaurants here are the worst.

Using -ísimo for emphasis

You can add -ísimo to the end of an adjective to make it stronger.

La chaqueta es carísima.
The jacket is very expensive.

El libro es malísimo.   The book is very bad.

La comida es riquísima.
The food is really delicious.

Don't forget to make adjectives agree!

Now try this

Complete the sentences with the correct comparative or superlative.

1 Este libro es .... de la trilogía. (*worst*)
2 Mis hermanos son .... amigos que tengo. (*best*)
3 La falda es .... de la tienda. (*prettiest*)
4 Este partido de fútbol es .... (*really boring*)
5 Carmen es .... jugadora. (*best*)
6 Este piso es .... que he visto hoy. (*ugliest*)
7 Lucas es .... que Juan. (*more sporty*)
8 Mi hermana es .... que mi hermano. (*funnier*)

Other adjectives

Here you can revise demonstrative adjectives and some useful indefinite adjectives.

Demonstrative adjectives

Demonstrative adjectives ('this', 'that', 'these', 'those') agree with their noun in number and gender.

	Masculine	Feminine	
Singular	este	esta	this
Plural	estos	estas	these
Singular	ese	esa	that
Plural	esos	esas	those

este móvil   this mobile
esa calculadora   that calculator
esos chicos   those boys
estas chicas   these girls

Using different words for 'that' and 'those'

In Spanish there are two words for 'that' / 'those': ese and aquel. You use aquel to refer to something further away.

esa chica y aquel chico
that girl and that boy
(over there)

	Masculine	Feminine	
Singular	aquel	aquella	that
Plural	aquellos	aquellas	those

Indefinite adjectives

Indefinite adjectives come up in a lot of contexts, so make sure you know how to use them.

cada   each
otro   another
todo   all
mismo   same
algún / alguna some / any

As with all other adjectives, remember to make them agree. Exception: **cada** – it doesn't change.

Quisiera otra cerveza.   I would like another beer.

Todos los pasajeros   All the passengers
  estaban enfadados.   were angry.

Llevamos la misma   We're wearing the
  camiseta.   same T-shirt.

¿Tienes algún   Do you have any
  cuaderno?   exercise books?

Cada estudiante puede   Each student can
  usar un ordenador.   use a computer.

Now try this

Translate into Spanish.
1 That boy is my cousin.
2 This apple is tasty.
3 I want to buy those jeans.
4 That house over there is really big.
5 This film is boring.
6 I don't want that jumper – I want that cardigan over there.

86

Pronouns

Use pronouns to avoid repeating nouns – it helps make your Spanish more fluent and interesting.

Subject, direct object and indirect object

- The **subject** is the person / thing doing the action (shown by the verb).
- The **object** is the person / thing having the action (shown by the verb) done to it.
  It can be **direct** or **indirect**.

Subject	Verb	Direct object	Indirect object
Marisa	sends	the email	to David.
She	sends	it	to him.

Subject pronoun		Direct object pronoun		Indirect object pronoun	
I	yo	me	me	(to / for) me	me
you	tú	you	te	(to / for) you	te
he / it	él	him / it	lo	(to / for) him / it	le
she / it	ella	her / it	la	(to / for) her / it	le
we	nosotros / as	us	nos	(to / for) us	nos
you	vosotros / as	you	os	(to / for) you	os
they	ellos / ellas	them	los / las	(to / for) them	les

Subject pronouns aren't often used in Spanish because the verb ending is enough to show who is doing the action. They're sometimes used for **emphasis**.

A mí me gusta Perú, pero él quiere ir a México.   I like Peru but he wants to go to Mexico.

Position of object pronouns

In general, object pronouns come:
- **before** the verb
- **after** a negative

La compré en el supermercado.	I bought it in the supermarket.
No la tengo.	I don't have it.
Nadie les escribe.	No one writes to them.

The object pronoun can be added to the infinitive in the near future tense.

Voy a comprarlo por Internet.   or

Lo voy a comprar por Internet.
I'm going to buy it online.

Object pronouns are attached to the end of a positive imperative.

¡Hazlo! Do it!

Now try this

Rewrite the sentences, replacing the words in bold with pronouns.
1 Voy a dar **el regalo** a mi padre.
2 Envío muchos mensajes **a mi hermana**.
3 Voy a comprar **un libro**.
4 Pon **los tomates** en la bolsa.
5 Quiero decir **a Rahul** un secreto.

The present tense

This page covers all three types of regular verb and radical-changing verbs in the present tense.

Present tense (regular)

To form the present tense of regular verbs, replace the infinitive ending as follows:

	hablar – to speak	comer – to eat	vivir – to live
I	hablo	como	vivo
you	hablas	comes	vives
he/she/it	habla	come	vive
we	hablamos	comemos	vivimos
you	habláis	coméis	vivís
they	hablan	comen	viven

How to use the present tense

Use the present tense to talk about:
• what you are doing **now**
• what you do **regularly**
• what things are **like**.

You can also use the present tense to talk about planned future events.

Mañana voy a España.   Tomorrow I'm going to Spain.

Remember that **usted** (polite / formal form of 'you') takes the endings for 'he / she / it'.
¿Habla inglés?   **Do you speak English?**

Radical-changing verbs

In radical-changing verbs, the vowel in the syllable before the infinitive ending changes in the singular and 3rd person plural. There are three common groups.

	o ➡ ue	e ➡ ie	e ➡ i
	poder to be able	querer to want	pedir to ask
I	puedo	quiero	pido
you	puedes	quieres	pides
he/she/it	puede	quiere	pide
we	podemos	queremos	pedimos
you	podéis	queréis	pedís
they	pueden	quieren	piden

Other examples of radical-changing verbs:

u/o ➡ ue	e ➡ ie
jugar ➡ juego to play	empezar ➡ empiezo to start
dormir ➡ duermo to sleep	entender ➡ entiendo to understand
volver ➡ vuelvo to return	pensar ➡ pienso to think
encontrar ➡ encuentro to meet	preferir ➡ prefiero to prefer

¿Quieres salir esta noche?
Do you want to go out tonight?
Rafa juega al tenis todos los días.
Rafa plays tennis every day.

Now try this

Complete the sentences using the present tense. Then translate the sentences into English.

1 No .... música clásica. *escuchar (I)*
2 Mis padres .... inglés. *hablar*
3 Mi amigo .... al baloncesto conmigo. *jugar*
4 ¿............... ir al cine conmigo esta noche? *querer (you singular informal)*
5 Siempre .... fruta para estar sanos. *comer (we)*
6 Siempre .... dinero en la calle. *encontrar (they)*
7 ¿............... en el campo? *vivir (you plural informal)*
8 Mi hermano .... en su propio dormitorio. *dormir*

Reflexive verbs (present)

Reflexive verbs include a reflexive pronoun which refers back to the person doing the action.

Present tense (regular)

Reflexive verbs have the same endings as other present tense verbs but contain a reflexive pronoun. Some are also radical-changing verbs.

	lavarse to wash	vestirse to get dressed
I	me lavo	me visto
you	te lavas	te vistes
he / she / it / you (polite)	se lava	se viste
we	nos lavamos	nos vestimos
you	os laváis	os vestís
they	se lavan	se visten

In the infinitive form, the pronoun can be added to the end of the verb.

Voy a levantarme.   I'm going to get up.

> You can use the reflexive pronoun se to create an impersonal construction:
> Aquí no se puede nadar.
> You cannot swim here.
> Se necesita gente con experiencia.
> People with experience are needed.

Useful reflexive verbs

Reflexive verbs are particularly useful when you describe your daily routines. They are also useful for describing some emotions.

acordarse de	me acuerdo de	I remember
arrepentirse de	me arrepiento de	I regret
bañarse	me baño	I take a bath
divertirse	me divierto	I enjoy myself
ducharse	me ducho	I take a shower
enfadarse	me enfado	I get angry
levantarse	me levanto	I get up
llamarse	me llamo	I am called
maquillarse	me maquillo	I put on make-up
parecerse a	me parezco a	I look like
pasearse	me paseo	I go for a walk
preocuparse	me preocupo	I worry
sentarse	me siento	I sit down
quejarse	me quejo	I complain

Nos vestimos.
We get dressed.

Mi hermana se cepilla los dientes.
My sister brushes her teeth.

Mis amigas se maquillan en casa.
My friends put on their make-up at home.

¿A qué hora te duchas?
What time do you take a shower?

Now try this

Complete the sentences with the correct reflexive pronouns.

1 .... despierto temprano.
2 Mi hermano .... afeita a las siete.
3 Mañana voy a peinar .... antes de desayunar.
4 .... acostamos siempre a la misma hora.
5 ¿A qué hora .... levantas normalmente?
6 Mis padres .... duchan después de desayunar.

89

Irregular verbs (present)

Make sure you know how to use these irregular verbs correctly.

The verbs ir and tener

These key verbs are irregular in the present tense.

	ir – to go
I	voy
you	vas
he / she / it / you (polite)	va
we	vamos
you	vais
they	van

	tener – to have
I	tengo
you	tienes
he / she / it / you (polite)	tiene
we	tenemos
you	tenéis
they	tienen

Tengo que hacer los deberes y luego voy al cine.
I have to do my homework and then I'm going to the cinema.

Other irregular verbs

Some other useful verbs are also irregular in the present tense.

decir – to say	digo, dices, dice, decimos, decís, dicen
oír – to hear	oigo, oyes, oye, oímos, oís, oyen
venir – to come	vengo, vienes, viene, venimos, venís, vienen

Some verbs are irregular to keep the pronunciation correct.
proteger – to protect ➡ protejo – I protect
coger – to take ➡ cojo – I take

Irregular 'I' forms

Some verbs are irregular in the 'I' form only.

conducir	to drive	➡ conduzco
conocer	to know / meet	➡ conozco
dar	to give	➡ doy
hacer	to make / do	➡ hago
poner	to put	➡ pongo
saber	to know	➡ sé
salir	to go out	➡ salgo
traer	to bring	➡ traigo

Now try this

Complete these sentences with the correct form of the verb in brackets. Then translate them into English.

1 Yo .... a las siete y media para ir al concierto. (*salir*)
2 Mis primos .... los ojos azules y son rubios. (*tener*)
3 Me gusta mucho ir a la playa pero no .... nadar. (*saber*)
4 Siempre .... el autobús cuando voy al instituto. (*coger*)
5 Mis amigos .... los deberes en la biblioteca pero yo los .... en casa. (*hacer*)
6 Creo que .... muy bien, ¡pero mi madre cree que no! (*conducir*)

Ser and *estar*

Spanish has two verbs meaning 'to be': ser and estar. Both are irregular – you need to know them well.

The present tense of ser

	ser – to be
I am	soy
you are	eres
he / she / it is	es
we are	somos
you are	sois
they are	son

Roberto es un chico feliz.
Roberto is a happy boy.

When to use ser

Use ser for **permanent** things.

- nationality

Soy galés.	I'm Welsh.

- occupation

Es profesor.	He's a teacher.

- colour and size

Es rojo. Es pequeño.	It's red. It's small.

- personality

Son habladoras.	They're talkative.

- telling the time

Son las tres.	It's three o'clock.

The present tense of estar

	estar – to be
I am	estoy
you are	estás
he / she / it is	está
we are	estamos
you are	estáis
they are	están

Hoy Alicia está aburridísima.
Alicia is really bored today.

When to use estar

Use estar for **temporary** things and **locations**.

- illness

Estoy enfermo.	I'm unwell.

- appearance (temporary)

Estás guapo.	You look handsome.

- feelings (temporary)

Estoy contento porque gané la lotería.
I'm happy because I won the lottery.

- location

Delhi está en India.	Delhi is in India.

Watch out for this one!
ser listo   to be clever
estar listo   to be ready

Now try this

Complete the sentences with **ser** or **estar** in the present tense.

1 ¿Dónde .... la parada de autobuses?
2 Valencia .... grande e interesante.
3 Mi hermana .... abogada.
4 .... constipado. *(I)*
5 Las botas .... negras.

6 Mi mejor amiga .... escocesa.
7 Hoy mis amigos no .... contentos porque tienen una prueba.
8 Mahmud .... guapo esta noche con su chaqueta nueva.

The gerund

Gerunds are '-ing' words. Use this page to review how they're formed and used.

The gerund

To form the gerund of regular verbs, replace the infinitive ending as follows:

hablar – hablando
comer – comiendo
vivir – viviendo

Common irregular gerunds:

caer	cayendo	falling
dormir	durmiendo	sleeping
leer	leyendo	reading
oír	oyendo	hearing
pedir	pidiendo	asking (for something)
poder	pudiendo	being able to
reír	riendo	laughing

> Está jugando al fútbol.
> She's playing football.

Uses of the gerund

You use the gerund:

- to give more information about how something was or is being done
  Voy andando al instituto.
  I go to school on foot.

- after ir (to go), seguir (to keep on) and continuar (to continue)
  Sigo aprendiendo informática porque es útil.
  I keep studying ICT because it's useful.

- to form the present continuous and imperfect continuous tenses (see below).

> You can't always translate an '-ing' verb in English by the gerund in Spanish, e.g.
> Aprender español es emocionante.
> **Learning Spanish is exciting.**
> Vamos a salir mañana.
> **We're leaving tomorrow.**

Present continuous tense

The present continuous describes what is happening at this moment:
present tense of estar + the gerund

	estar – to be	gerund
I	estoy	
you	estás	haciendo
he / she / it	está	saliendo
we	estamos	durmiendo
you	estáis	riendo
they	están	

Estoy viendo la televisión. I'm watching TV.

Imperfect continous tense

This tense describes what was happening at a certain moment in the past:
imperfect tense of estar + the gerund

	estar – to be	gerund
I	estaba	
you	estabas	visitando
he / she / it	estaba	estudiando
we	estábamos	escribiendo
you	estabais	buscando
they	estaban	

Estaba leyendo.   I was reading.

Now try this

Rewrite the sentences using the present continuous tense. Write them again using the imperfect continuous.

1 Juego al tenis.
2 Escribo un correo electrónico.
3 Habla con mi amigo Juan.
4 Duerme en la cama.
5 Como cereales.
6 Tomo el sol en la playa.
7 Navegan por Internet.
8 ¿Cantas en tu habitación?

The preterite tense

The preterite tense is used to talk about completed actions in the past.

Preterite tense (regular)

To form the preterite tense of regular verbs, replace the infinitive ending as follows:

	hablar – to speak	comer – to eat	vivir – to live
I	hablé	comí	viví
you	hablaste	comiste	viviste
he / she / it	habló	comió	vivió
we	hablamos	comimos	vivimos
you	hablasteis	comisteis	vivisteis
they	hablaron	comieron	vivieron

> Be careful – accents can be significant.
> Hablo. I speak.
> Habló. He / She spoke.

Preterite tense (irregular)

	ir – to go ser – to be	hacer – to do	ver – to see
I	fui	hice	vi
you	fuiste	hiciste	viste
he / she / it	fue	hizo	vio
we	fuimos	hicimos	vimos
you	fuisteis	hicisteis	visteis
they	fueron	hicieron	vieron

> The verbs **ir** and **ser** have the same forms in the preterite. Use context to work out which is meant.

How to use the preterite tense

You use the preterite to describe completed actions in the past.

El año pasado viajé a Estados Unidos.
Last year I travelled to the United States.

> Recognise and use a range of preterite tense time expressions.
>
> | | |
> |---|---|
> | ayer | yesterday |
> | anoche | last night |
> | anteayer / antes de ayer | the day before yesterday |
> | el verano pasado | last summer |
> | la semana pasada | last week |

Useful irregular preterite forms to know:

andar	anduve	I walked
dar	di	I gave
decir	dije	I said
estar	estuve	I was
poner	puse	I put
saber	supe	I knew
tener	tuve	I had
venir	vine	I came

> Note these verbs with irregular spelling in 'I' form only:
>
> | cruzar | crucé | I crossed |
> |---|---|---|
> | empezar | empecé | I started |
> | jugar | jugué | I played |
> | llegar | llegué | I arrived |
> | tocar | toqué | I played |

Now try this

Identify the tense in each sentence (present or preterite).
Then translate the sentences into English.

1 Voy a Italia.
2 Llegué a las seis.
3 Navego por Internet.
4 Escuchó música.
5 Fue a una fiesta que fue guay.
6 Hizo frío y llovió un poco.
7 Vimos a Pablo en el mercado.
8 Jugué al baloncesto en la playa.

The imperfect tense

The imperfect is another verb tense used to talk about the past.

Imperfect tense (regular)

To form the imperfect tense of regular verbs, replace the infinitive ending as follows:

	hablar – to speak	comer – to eat	vivir – to live
I	hablaba	comía	vivía
you	hablabas	comías	vivías
he / she / it	hablaba	comía	vivía
we	hablábamos	comíamos	vivíamos
you	hablabais	comíais	vivíais
they	hablaban	comían	vivían

-er and -ir verbs have the same endings.

Try to use both the **imperfect** and the **preterite** in your work to aim for a higher grade.

How to use the imperfect tense

You use the imperfect to talk about:
- what people used to do / how things used to be

Antes no separaba la basura.
I didn't use to sort the rubbish before.

- repeated actions in the past

Jugaba al tenis todos los días.
I played tennis every day.

- descriptions in the past

El hotel era caro.
The hotel was expensive.

Hacía de canguro. Ahora trabajo como jardinero.
I used to babysit. Now I work as a gardener.

Imperfect tense (irregular)

Only three verbs are irregular:

	ir – to go	ser – to be	ver – to see
I	iba	era	veía
you	ibas	eras	veías
he / she / it	iba	era	veía
we	íbamos	éramos	veíamos
you	ibais	erais	veíais
they	iban	eran	veían

Preterite or imperfect?

- Use the preterite tense for a **single / completed** event in the past.
- Use the imperfect tense for **repeated / continuous** events in the past.

En Brighton había un castillo.
There used to be a castle in Brighton.
Ayer visité Brighton.
Yesterday I visited Brighton.

Now try this

Complete the sentences with the imperfect or preterite tense, as appropriate.

1 Mi madre .... para Iberia todos los veranos. *trabajar*
2 Ayer .... mucho chocolate. *comer (I)*
3 Antes .... a Grecia a menudo con mis padres. *ir (I)*
4 En los años setenta .... más paro que ahora. *haber*
5 El verano pasado .... Marruecos por primera vez. *visitar (I)*
6 De pequeño mi hermanito .... siempre. *llorar*

The future tense

To aim for a higher grade, you need to use a future tense as well as the present and past.

Future tense

To form the future tense of most verbs, add the following endings to the infinitive:

ir – to go			
I	iré	we	iremos
you	irás	you	iréis
he / she / it	irá	they	irán

Some verbs use a different stem. You need to memorise these:

decir to say ➡ diré I will say
haber there is / are ➡ habrá there will be
hacer to make / do ➡ haré I will make / do
poder to be able to ➡ podré I will be able to
querer to want ➡ querré I will want
saber to know ➡ sabré I will know
salir to leave ➡ saldré I will leave
tener to have ➡ tendré I will have
venir to come ➡ vendré I will come

Immediate future tense

You form the immediate future tense as follows:
present tense of ir + a + infinitive

	ir – to go		infinitive
I	voy		
you	vas		
he / she / it	va	a	mandar bailar salir venir
we	vamos		
you	vais		
they	van		

¿Vas a comer algo?
Are you going to have something to eat?

Vamos a ir a la fiesta.
We're going to go to the festival.

Recognise and use a range of time expressions that indicate the future,
e.g. mañana   tomorrow,   mañana por la mañana   tomorrow morning,
el mes que viene   next month,   el próximo viernes   next Friday.

Using the future tense

Use the future tense to talk about what will happen in the future.

El año que viene será difícil encontrar un buen trabajo.
Next year it will be difficult to find a good job.
Si trabajo como voluntario, mejoraré el mundo.
If I work as a volunteer, I will make the world better.

Using the immediate future tense

You use the immediate future tense to say what is going to happen. It is used to talk about future plans.

En Barcelona va a comprar recuerdos.
He's going to buy souvenirs in Barcelona.
Voy a salir esta tarde.
I'm going to go out this afternoon.

Now try this

1 Rewrite the sentences using the future tense.
  (a) Nunca fumo.
  (b) Ayudo a los demás.
  (c) Cambiamos el mundo.
  (d) Trabajo en un aeropuerto.

2 Rewrite the sentences using the immediate future tense.
  (a) Salgo a las seis.
  (b) Soy médico.
  (c) Va a Pakistán.
  (d) Mañana juego al tenis.

95

The conditional tense

The conditional is used to describe what you **would do** or what **would happen** in the future.

The conditional

To form the conditional, you add the following endings to the infinitive:

	hablar – to speak
I	hablaría
you	hablarías
he / she / it	hablaría
we	hablaríamos
you	hablaríais
they	hablarían

The endings are the same for ALL verbs.

Some verbs use a different stem.

decir to say	→	diría
haber there is / are	→	habría
hacer to do	→	haría
poder to be able to	→	podría
querer to want	→	querría
saber to know	→	sabría
salir to leave	→	saldría
tener to have	→	tendría
venir to come	→	vendría

Un sistema de alquiler de bicicletas sería una idea muy buena.
A bike hire scheme would be a really good idea.

Use poder in the conditional + the infinitive to say what you **could** do.
Podríamos ir a Ibiza.   We could go to Ibiza.

Use deber in the conditional + the infinitive to say what you **should** do.
Debería fumar menos cigarrillos.
I should smoke fewer cigarettes.

Expressing future intent

The conditional can be used to express future intent.
Use gustar in the conditional + the infinitive.
En el futuro ...

Me gustaría ir a Australia.
I'd like to go to Australia.

Me gustaría ser bailarín.
I'd like to be a dancer.

Me gustaría comprarme un coche nuevo.
I'd like to buy a new car.

You can also use me encantaría, e.g. Me encantaría ser futbolista.

Now try this

Rewrite the text, changing the verbs in bold to the conditional.
Para mantenerme en forma **bebo** mucha agua. **Hago** mucho ejercicio y **practico** mucho deporte. Nunca **tomo** drogas y no **bebo** alcohol. **Como** mucha fruta y **me acuesto** temprano – siempre **duermo** ocho horas, gracias a eso **llevo** una vida sana.

Perfect and pluperfect

The perfect and pluperfect are two more tenses used to talk about the past. You should be able to use both.

Perfect tense

To form the perfect tense, use the present tense of haber + past participle:

	haber – to have
I	he
you	has
he / she / it	ha
we	hemos
you	habéis
they	han

Pluperfect tense

To form the pluperfect tense, use the imperfect tense of haber + past participle:

	haber – to have
I	había
you	habías
he / she / it	había
we	habíamos
you	habíais
they	habían

Past participle

To form the past participle, replace the infinitive ending as follows:

hablar ➡ hablado
comer ➡ comido
vivir ➡ vivido

Ha descargado una nueva peli.   He has downloaded a new film.

No habían salido.   They hadn't gone out.
Había hecho mis deberes.   I had done my homework.
¿Has visto a María?   Have you seen María?

Here are some common irregular past participles:

abrir	➡	abierto	opened
decir	➡	dicho	said
escribir	➡	escrito	written
hacer	➡	hecho	done
poner	➡	puesto	put
romper	➡	roto	broken
ver	➡	visto	seen
volver	➡	vuelto	returned

Using the perfect tense

The perfect tense describes what someone **has done** or something that **has happened**.

He ido a la piscina.
I have been to the swimming pool.

Using the pluperfect tense

The pluperfect tense describes what someone **had done** or something that **had happened** at a particular time in the past.

Cuando llegó, la orquesta había empezado ya.
When he arrived, the orchestra had already started.

Now try this

Rewrite the sentences in the correct order. Identify the tense in each one: perfect or pluperfect?

1 visitado / he / . / novio / mi / con / Palma
2 ayuda / hecho / deberes / mi / . / han / sus / con
3 ido / . / habíamos / Adel / con / supermercado / al
4 amor / de / carta / una / . / escrito / ha / hermana / mi
5 has / ¿ / abrigo / mi / visto / ?
6 llegó / cuando / , / primos / ya / comido / . / mis / habían

Giving instructions

You use the imperative to give instructions and commands.

The imperative

The imperative changes its form depending on two things:
• whether the command is positive or negative
• who receives the command.

Toma la primera calle a la izquierda.   Take the first street on the left.
Poned la mesa.   Lay the table.
No tiréis basura al suelo.   Don't throw litter on the floor.

> Commands may be given to one person (singular) or more than one person (plural). They may also be informal or formal.

Positive commands

The tú command (informal singular) is formed by removing the -s from the tú form of the present tense.

Infinitive	Tú present tense	Tú imperative
hablar	hablas	habla
comer	comes	come
vivir	vives	vive

The vosotros command (informal plural) is formed by taking the infinitive, removing the -r and adding -d.

Infinitive	Vosotros imperative
hablar	hablad
comer	comed
vivir	vivid

To give a **formal** command (usted or ustedes forms), you **always** use the present subjunctive. For information on how to form the present subjunctive, go to page 99.

¡No hable!   Don't speak! (usted form)
¡Coman!   Eat! (ustedes form)

Irregular imperatives

These verbs have irregular tú forms in the imperative.

decir	➡ ¡Di!	Say!
hacer	➡ ¡Haz!	Do!
ir	➡ ¡Ve!	Go!
dar	➡ ¡Da!	Give!
salir	➡ ¡Sal!	Leave!
tener	➡ ¡Ten!	Have!

Negative commands

You use the present subjunctive to form **all** negative commands. For more information on the present subjunctive, go to page 99.

¡No grites!   Don't shout! (tú form)
¡No habléis!   Don't talk! (vosotros form)
¡No fume!   Don't smoke! (usted form)
¡No beban!   Don't drink! (ustedes form)

¡No saques fotos!

Now try this

Translate the instructions into English.
1 Escríbeme.
2 Espera a tu hermana.
3 No me digas nada.
4 ¡No gritéis!
5 Haz clic aquí.
6 ¡No saques fotos!
7 Contestad las preguntas.
8 No lo dejes todo para el último momento.

No destruyan la selva.

The present subjunctive

The subjunctive form of the verb is used in certain constructions.

The present subjunctive

To form the present subjunctive, replace the -o ending of the 'I' form of the present tense as follows:

	hablar – to speak	comer – to eat	vivir – to live
I	hable	coma	viva
you	hables	comas	vivas
he / she / it	hable	coma	viva
we	hablemos	comamos	vivamos
you	habléis	comáis	viváis
they	hablen	coman	vivan

-er and -ir verbs have the same endings.

This rule works for most verbs which are irregular in the present tense.

Infinitive	Present	Subjunctive
hacer	hago	haga
tener	tengo	tenga

Two verbs, ir and ser, are different.

	ir – to go	ser – to be
I	vaya	sea
you	vayas	seas
he / she / it	vaya	sea
we	vayamos	seamos
you	vayáis	seáis
they	vayan	sean

How to use the subjunctive

The subjunctive is used:

* to express doubt or uncertainty

No creo que tenga tiempo.
I don't think I have time.

* to deny that information is true

No es verdad que sea adicto al ordenador.
It isn't true that I'm a computer addict.

* after ojalá

¡Ojalá (que) nadie me vea!
Let's hope no one sees me!

* after cuando when talking about the future

Cuando sea mayor, quiero hacer caída libre.
When I'm older, I want to do skydiving.

* to express a wish with querer que

¿Quieres que nos vayamos?
Do you want us to go?

Remember: the subjunctive is also used in some imperatives – see page 98.

Now try this

Translate the sentences into English.
1 Cuando vaya a la universidad, estudiaré francés.
2 No creo que tu amigo sea guapo.
3 Cuando tenga dieciocho años, me tomaré un año sabático.
4 Quiero que hables con Pablo.
5 No es verdad que mi ropa sea horrible.
6 No creo que Italia sea el mejor equipo de fútbol.

It's important you can **recognise** the subjunctive. If you're really aiming high, you could also try to **use** a few subjunctive forms in your writing and speaking.

Negatives

You need to be able to understand and use negatives in all parts of the exam.

Negatives

no	not
no ... nada	nothing / not anything
no ... nunca	never
no ... jamás	never
no ... ni ... ni ...	not ... (either) ... or ...
no ... tampoco	not ... either
no ... ningún / ninguna	no / not any
no ... nadie	no one

How to use negatives

- The simplest way to make a sentence negative in Spanish is to use no. It comes before the verb.
  No nadé en el mar.
  I didn't swim in the sea.
- Negative expressions with two parts sandwich the verb (i.e. they go round it).
  Dicen que no nieva nunca en Málaga.
  They say that it never snows in Malaga.
- Two-part negative expressions can be shortened and put before the verb for emphasis.
  Nadie está aquí. No one's here.

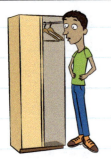

No tengo nada que ponerme.
I don't have anything to wear.

No quiero ni nadar ni hacer yoga.
I don't want to swim or do yoga.

No me gustan los perros tampoco.
I don't like dogs either.

Expressions to use with negatives

Ya no estudio alemán.	I no longer study German.
No bebo agua sino zumo de naranja.	I don't drink water but orange juice.
Todavía no ha estudiado mucho.	He hasn't studied a lot yet.
Espero que no.	I hope not.
Creo que no.	I don't think so.
Claro que no.	Of course not.

Use a range of negatives in your Spanish to aim for a higher grade.

Now try this

Make the sentences negative, giving the opposite meanings. Then translate the original sentences into English.
1 Siempre como verduras.
2 Tengo un libro.
3 Conozco a todos sus amigos.
4 Todo el mundo juega al baloncesto.
5 Siempre hago mis deberes.
6 Me gusta navegar por Internet y descargar música.
7 Tiene todo.
8 Tengo muchos amigos en Londres.

Special verbs

Verbs like gustar are used mainly in the 3rd person. You'll need them for a lot of topics, so they're worth learning carefully.

Present tense of gustar

Me gusta ('I like') literally translates as 'it pleases me'. The thing that does the pleasing (i.e. the thing I like) is the subject.
Me gusta este libro.   I like this book.
If the subject is plural, use me gustan.
Me gustan estos libros.
I like these books.
The pronoun changes as follows:

me	gusta(n)	I like
te	gusta(n)	you like
le	gusta(n)	he / she / it likes
nos	gusta(n)	we like
os	gusta(n)	you like
les	gusta(n)	they like

To talk about other people's likes / dislikes, you need a before their name:
A Ignacio le gusta el deporte. Ignacio likes sport.

Preterite tense of gustar

In the preterite:
me gusta ➡ me gustó
me gustan ➡ me gustaron
The pronouns in the other forms are the same as for the present tense.
Nos gustó la comida india.
We liked Indian food.
Le gustaron las tiendas.
He liked the shops.

If you're aiming for higher grades, use gustar in the preterite to extend your language range.

encantar behaves in the same way as gustar:
Le encanta la música rock. He loves rock music.

Other verbs like gustar

Other verbs follow the same pattern as gustar: pronoun + 3rd person singular / plural of the verb

doler	me duele(n)	My ... hurt(s)
quedar	me queda(n)	I have ... left
hacer falta	me hace(n) falta	I need ...
faltar	me falta	I'm missing ...

Me duele el tobillo.
My ankle hurts.

Les quedan 20 euros.
They have 20 euros left.
¿Te hace falta una cuchara?
Do you need a spoon?
Le faltan dos libros.
He's missing two books.

Now try this

Complete the sentences.
1 .... el brazo. *(doler, I)*
2 .... el queso. *(gustar, she)*
3 .... las fresas. *(gustar, I, preterite)*
4 .... un cuchillo. *(hacer falta, they)*
5 .... los pies. *(doler, he)*
6 .... el mandarín. *(encantar, I)*
7 .... cinco euros. *(quedar, we)*
8 .... las películas francesas. *(gustar, María)*

101

Por and para

Por and para are both often translated by 'for' in English. Learn the different contexts in which they're used.

Using por

You use por for:

- **cause**
  Pagué cien euros por el vuelo.
  I paid €100 for the flight.
  El vuelo fue cancelado por la huelga.
  The flight was cancelled because of the strike.

- action **on behalf of** someone
  Lo hizo por mí.   She did it for me.

- **rates**
  Gano seis euros por hora.
  I earn €6 per hour.

- means of **communication**
  Me llamó por teléfono.
  He called me on the phone.

- unspecified periods of **time**
  Me quedaré en Toronto por poco tiempo.
  I will stay in Toronto for a short time.

Using para

You use para for:

- **purpose** (it can often be translated by 'in order to')
  Llevamos una botella de agua fría para el viaje.
  We're taking a bottle of cold water for the journey.
  Voy a utilizar mi tarjeta de crédito para pagar el hotel.
  I'm going to use my credit card to pay for the hotel.
  Voy a comprar unos regalos para mi familia.
  I'm going to buy some presents for my family.

- **destination**
  Ha salido para Amsterdam.
  She has left for Amsterdam.

- specific **time** periods or **deadlines** in the future
  Quisiera una habitación para quince días.
  I would like a room for a fortnight.

Try writing out phrases with **por** and **para**, using one colour for **por** each time and another colour for **para**. Then when you're trying to remember which one to use, try to visualise the colour.

Now try this

1 Choose **por** or **para** to complete these sentences.

(a) Voy a ir a la ciudad .... hacer compras.

(b) El tren .... São Paulo sale a las seis.

(c) Gracias .... el regalo.

(d) Los deberes son .... mañana.

(e) Este regalo es .... mi profesor.

(f) Voy a llamarle .... teléfono.

(g) Una azafata gana veinte euros .... hora.

2 Tick the sentences which are correct. Correct those that are wrong.

(a) Salimos por Nueva York.

(b) Solo estudio para la mañana.

(c) Por ganar hay que trabajar duro.

(d) Voy a hacerlo para ti.

(e) Juego al fútbol para divertirme.

(f) Estas flores son por mi novia.

(g) Gano dinero para comprar un movíl nuevo.

(h) En el 18 por ciento por ciento de las casas hay una motocicleta.

Questions and exclamations

Being able to use questions and exclamations is essential in most topics.

How to ask questions

To ask yes / no questions, use the same language as you would to say the sentence and:
• if you're writing, add question marks
• if you're speaking, use a rising intonation at the end.

¿Estudias español?
Do you study Spanish?
¿Quieres ir al polideportivo?
Do you want to go to the leisure centre?

> Remember the ¿ at the start.

To ask open questions, use a question word.

¿Cuándo?	When?
¿Dónde?	Where?
¿Adónde?	Where to?
¿De dónde?	From where?
¿Cuánto / a?	How much?
¿Cuántos / as?	How many?
¿Qué?	What?
¿Por qué?	Why?
¿Cómo?	How?
¿Cuál(es)?	Which (ones)?
¿Quién(es)?	Who?
¿Cuál (de estos libros) te gusta más?	Which (one of these books) do you like more?

> Don't forget the accents on question words.

Using exclamations

Using exclamations is a good way to extend how you give opinions in your spoken and written Spanish. Here are some useful examples:

¡Qué lástima!	What a shame!
¡Qué problema!	What a problem!
¡Qué raro!	How strange!
¡Qué va!	No way!
¡Qué rollo!	How boring!

> Remember the ¡ at the start as well as at the end.

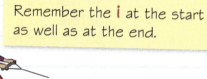

¡Qué emocionante!
How exciting!

¡Qué difícil!
How difficult!

Question tag

English has a lot of different ways of asking for confirmation, e.g. 'doesn't he?', 'haven't they?', 'can't you?'. In Spanish it's much easier. You just put verdad at the end of a question.
¿Pablo es tu novio, verdad?
Pablo is your boyfriend, isn't he?

Now try this

Match the sentence halves.

1 ¿Cuál   a cuesta?
2 ¿Adónde   b personas hay en tu clase?
3 ¿Quién   c te llamas?
4 ¿Dónde   d es tu asignatura preferida?
5 ¿Cuánto   e está Jaén?
6 ¿Cuántas   f fuiste de vacaciones el año pasado?
7 ¿Cómo   g es tu cumpleaños?
8 ¿Cuándo   h es tu cantante preferido?

Connectives and adverbs

Use connectives to link phrases and sentences, and use adverbs to add detail to your Spanish.

Connectives

Connectives are words that link phrases and sentences together. You can use them to make your Spanish more varied and interesting.

Hago atletismo pero no me gusta mucho.
I do athletics but I don't like it much.

además	as well / besides
antes (de)	before
así que	so / therefore
después (de)	after
entonces	then
mientras	while
o	or
pero	but
por desgracia	unfortunately
por eso	therefore
por una parte	on the one hand
por otra parte	on the other hand
porque	because
pues	then
si	if
sin embargo	however
también	also
y	and

Another good way to improve your work is to extend your sentences using clauses with: que that / who, donde where, cuando when, como like / as, cuyo whose.

Adverbs

Adverbs describe how an action is done – they give you more detail about verbs. Many adverbs are formed by adding -mente to the feminine form of the adjective

lento ➡ lenta ➡ lentamente   slowly

Adverbs usually come **after** the verb.

Monta a caballo frecuentemente.
She goes riding frequently.

Sometimes they come **before** the verb, for emphasis.

Irregular adverbs

Here are some useful irregular adverbs to learn:

bastante	enough	despacio	slowly
bien	well	mal	badly
demasiado	too	mucho	a lot
	much	poco	a little
deprisa	fast	ya	already

Siempre nado los martes.
I always go swimming on Tuesdays.

Now try this

1 Connect the sentence pairs with an appropriate connective.
   (a) Nunca voy al teatro. Es aburrido.
   (b) Jugaba al baloncesto. Juan hacía patinaje.
   (c) Estudiar. Iré a la universidad.
   (d) Nos gustaría ir a la playa. Está lloviendo.

2 Make adverbs from the adjectives. Translate them into English.
   (a) tranquilo
   (b) perfecto
   (c) difícil
   (d) severo

Numbers

Numbers come up in almost **every** context. Make sure you know them well.

Numbers

1	uno	11	once	21	veintiuno	100	cien
2	dos	12	doce	22	veintidós	101	ciento uno
3	tres	13	trece	30	treinta	200	doscientos / as
4	cuatro	14	catorce	31	treinta y uno	333	trescientos / as
5	cinco	15	quince	32	treinta y dos		treinta y tres
6	seis	16	dieciséis	40	cuarenta	1000	mil
7	siete	17	diecisiete	50	cincuenta		
8	ocho	18	dieciocho	60	sesenta		
9	nueve	19	diecinueve	70	setenta		
10	diez	20	veinte	80	ochenta		
				90	noventa		

> Numbers ending in uno need to agree. They drop the -o before a masculine noun: veintiún años

> The pattern for 31, 32, etc., is the same for 41, 42, etc.

> The hundreds need to agree. Note: there are some irregular forms:
> 500 – quinientos,
> 700 – setecientos,
> 900 – novecientos.

Ordinal numbers

When used with nouns, ordinal numbers agree.

primero	first	sexto	sixth
segundo	second	séptimo	seventh
tercero	third	octavo	eighth
cuarto	fourth	noveno	ninth
quinto	fifth	décimo	tenth

Primero and tercero change to primer and tercer before a masculine singular noun, e.g. el tercer día.

> Ordinals are NOT used for dates except for the 1st.

> You don't use a capital letter for the months.

Telling the time

Son las cinco.	It's five o'clock.
A las diez.	At ten o'clock.

> One o'clock is different: Es la una.

3.05	las tres y cinco
3.15	las tres y cuarto
3.30	las tres y media
3.45	las cuatro menos cuarto
3.55	las cuatro menos cinco

Dates

Dates follow this pattern:

13 December 1978 =

el trece de diciembre de mil novecientos setenta y ocho

21 July 2016

el veintiuno de julio del dos mil dieciséis

The first of the month can be either:

el primero de abril or el uno de abril.

Now try this

Write the numbers, dates and times in Spanish.

1 8.40 **2** 465 **3** 12 June 2014 **4** 7th **5** 11.30 **6** 76 **7** 1 January 1997 **8** 3rd

Vocabulary

This section starts with general terms that are useful in a wide variety of situations and then divides vocabulary into groups under the five main topics covered in this revision guide:

1 High-frequency language   **2** Identity and culture   **3** Local area, holiday and travel

4 School   **5** Future aspirations, study and work   **6** International and global dimension

Sections marked **Aiming Higher** are only needed if you are studying for the Higher tier paper.

Learning vocabulary is essential preparation for all four skills of reading, writing, listening and speaking but don't try to learn too much at once – concentrate on learning and testing yourself one page at a time.

1 High-frequency language

Verbs A–C

abrir	to open
acabar	to finish
aceptar	to accept
acompañar	to accompany
aconsejar	to advise
agradecer	to thank
ahorrar	to save (money)
almorzar	to have lunch
alquilar	to rent, hire
amar	to love
andar	to walk
añadir	to add
aprender	to learn
aprovechar	to take advantage of
arreglar	to tidy
averiguar	to check
ayudar	to help
bailar	to dance
bajar de	to get off (a bus)
beber	to drink
buscar	to look for
caer	to fall
cambiar	to change
cantar	to sing
cenar	to have dinner
cerrar	to close
coger	to take
comenzar	to start
comer	to eat
compartir	to share
comprar	to buy
conducir	to drive
conocer	to know (be familiar with)
contestar	to answer, reply
correr	to run
creer	to believe
cuidar	to look after
charlar	to chat

Verbs D–G

dar	to give
darse cuenta de	to realise
darse prisa	to hurry
deber	to have to
decir	to say
dejar	to leave (an object)
desayunar	to have breakfast
descargar (música)	to download (music)
desear	to wish
dibujar	to draw
dirigir	to manage, run, direct
discutir	to discuss
disfrutar de	to enjoy
divertirse	to enjoy oneself
doler	to hurt
dormir	to sleep
ducharse	to shower
durar	to last
echar de menos (a)	to miss
elegir	to choose
empezar	to begin
encantar (a)	to love
encontrar	to meet
enfadarse	to get angry
enseñar	to show, teach
entender	to understand
enviar	to send
equivocarse	to make a mistake
escribir	to write
escuchar	to listen
esperar	to hope, wait for
estar resfriado	to have a cold
estar	to be
evitar	to avoid
faltar	to be missing
ganar	to win, earn
gastar	to spend (money)
golpear	to hit
gustar (a)	to like

Verbs H–P

haber	to have (auxiliary verb)
hablar	to speak
hacer	to do, make
ir de compras	to go shopping
ir	to go
lavar(se)	to wash (oneself)
leer	to read
levantarse	to get up
llamar	to call
llamarse	to be called
llegar	to arrive
llevar	to carry, wear
llevarse bien con	to get on well with
llorar	to cry
llover	to rain
jugar	to play
mandar	to send
montar (a caballo)	to ride (a horse)
morir	to die
nacer	to be born
nadar	to swim
navegar en Internet	to surf the internet
nevar	to snow
odiar	to hate
ofrecer (regalos)	to give (presents)
oír	to hear
olvidar	to forget
parar(se)	to stop
parecer	to seem
pasar	to spend (time)
pasear(se)	to go for a walk
patinar	to skate
pedir	to ask (for)
pensar	to think
perder	to lose
poder	to be able to
poner	to put
preferir	to prefer
preguntar	to ask (a question)

Now try this

How accurate are your verbs? Pick three verbs from each column. For each verb, write out the full conjugation for the present, preterite and future tenses.

① High-frequency language

Verbs Q–V

quedarse	to stay, remain
quejarse	to complain
querer	to like, want
quitar la mesa	to clear the table
recordar	to remember
reembolsar	to refund
reír	to laugh
rellenar (una ficha)	to fill out (a form)
repasar	to revise
robar	to steal
romper	to break
saber	to know (a fact)
sacar (buenas) notas	to get (good) marks
sacar entradas	to buy tickets
sacar fotos	to take photographs
salir	to leave
saltar	to jump
seguir	to follow, continue
sentarse	to sit down
ser	to be
sonreír	to smile
subir	to climb, go up
tener	to have
tener calor / frío	to be hot / cold
tener éxito	to be successful
tener hambre	to be hungry
tener prisa	to be in a hurry
tener que	to have to
tener sed	to be thirsty
tener sueño	to be sleepy, tired
tener suerte	to be lucky
tirar	to throw
tirar de	to pull
tocar	to play (a musical instrument)
tomar	to take
tomar el sol	to sunbathe
torcer	to twist
trabajar	to work
traer	to bring
tratar de	to try to
triunfar	to succeed
utilizar	to use
vender	to sell
venir	to come
ver	to see
vestirse	to get dressed
vivir	to live

Adjectives A–J

abierto/a	open
aburrido/a	bored, boring
activo/a	active
agradecido/a	grateful
alegre	happy, cheerful
alto/a	high, tall
amable	kind
animado/a	lively
antiguo/a	former, old
antipático/a	unpleasant
asqueroso/a	disgusting
breve	brief
brillante	brilliant
bueno/a	good
buscado/a	sought after
caliente	hot
cansado/a	tired, tiring
castaño	chestnut brown
cercano/a	close
cerrado/a	closed
cómodo/a	comfortable
corto/a	short
de buen humor	in a good mood
débil	weak
delgado/a	slim
delicioso/a	delicious
deportista	sporty
difícil	difficult
divertido/a	amusing, fun
duro/a	hard
emocionante	exciting
enfadado/a	angry
estricto/a	strict
estupendo/a	great
entusiasmado/a	excited
fácil	easy
feo/a	ugly
fuerte	strong
gordo/a	fat
gran	great
grande	big, tall
gratis	free
guapo/a	handsome, pretty
guay	cool
hermoso/a	beautiful
horrible	awful
igual	same
increíble	unbelievable
joven	young
juntos/as	together

Adjectives L–V

largo/a	long
libre	free
ligero/a	light
limpio/a	clean
listo/a	ready, clever
lleno/a	full
maduro/a	mature
magnífico/a	magnificent
maravilloso/a	marvellous
mismo/a	same
necesario/a	necessary
numeroso/a	numerous
otro/a	other
pequeño/a	small
perdido/a	lost
perezoso/a	lazy
perfecto/a	perfect
pesado/a	heavy
podrido/a	rotten
preferido/a	favourite
propio/a	own
próximo/a	next
rápido/a	fast, quick
responsable	responsible
rico/a	rich, delicious
roto/a	broken
ruidoso/a	noisy
sabio/a	wise
sano/a	healthy
satisfecho/a	satisfied
sensacional	sensational
serio/a	serious
severo/a	strict
silencioso/a	silent
simpático/a	likeable
solo/a	alone, lonely
sucio/a	dirty
tímido/a	shy
todo/a	all
tonto/a	silly
trabajador(a)	hardworking
tradicional	traditional
travieso/a	naughty
último/a	last, latest
útil	useful
válido/a	valid
valiente	brave
valioso/a	valuable
verdadero/a	true
viejo/a	old

Now try this

Choose 5 positive adjectives and 5 negative ones from this page. Write 10 sentences in Spanish using a different adjective in each.

① High-frequency language

Adverbs

a menudo	often
a veces	sometimes
abajo	below (down)
afortunadamente	fortunately
ahí	over there
allí	there
aquí	here
arriba	up there
bastante	rather, quite
bien	well
casi	almost
demasiado	too
de prisa	quickly
desafortunadamente	unfortunately
desgraciadamente	unfortunately
durante mucho tiempo	for a long time
en seguida	straight away
especialmente	especially
inmediatamente	immediately
mal	badly
más	more
muy	very
otra vez	again
por suerte	luckily
quizás, quizá	perhaps
rápidamente	quickly
realmente	really
recientemente	recently
siempre	always
sobre todo	especially
todavía	still (yet)
ya	already

Connecting words

antes	before
aunque	though
después, luego	then, afterwards
entonces	then
lo primero (de todo)	first (of all)
o / u	or
pero	but
pues	so
sin embargo	however
también	also
y / e	and

Time expressions

a partir de	from
a tiempo	on time
ahora	now
ahora mismo	just now, straight away
al día siguiente	the next day
anoche	last night
anteayer	the day before yesterday
año (m)	year
año pasado	last year
ayer	yesterday
cada día	every day
de vez en cuando	from time to time
desde	since, from
día (m)	day
fin de semana (m)	weekend
hace	ago
hoy	today
luego	later
mañana	tomorrow
mañana (f)	morning
más tarde	later
noche (f)	night
pasado mañana	the day after tomorrow
pasado/a	last
por la mañana	in the morning
por la noche	at night
por la tarde	in the afternoon / evening
pronto	soon
próximo/a	next
puntual	on time
quince días	a fortnight
quincena (f)	a fortnight
semana (f)	week
siempre	always
siguiente	next
tarde (f)	afternoon, evening
temprano	early
todos los días	every day

Times

Son las dos y media

Son las tres menos cuarto

a la una	at one o'clock
a las dos	at two o'clock
a medianoche	at midnight
a mediodía	at noon
de la mañana	in the morning
de la noche	at night
de la tarde	in the afternoon / evening
es la una	it's one o'clock
hora (f)	hour
menos cuarto	quarter to
menos diez, etc.	ten to, etc.
minuto (m)	minute
son las dos, etc.	it's two o'clock, etc.
y cinco, etc.	five past, etc.
y cuarto	quarter past
y media	half past

Seasons

primavera (f)	spring
verano (m)	summer
otoño (m)	autumn
invierno (m)	winter

Colours

castaño	chestnut brown
claro/a	light
moreno/a	dark (hair, skin)
oscuro/a	dark
rubio/a	fair (hair, skin)
amarillo/a	
azul	
blanco/a	
gris	
marrón	
naranja	
negro/a	
rojo/a	
rosa	
verde	
violeta	

Now try this

Test yourself on the time expressions above by covering up the English column and then writing down the English translation yourself. Compare your answers with the list above. How many have you got right?

1 High-frequency language

Months of the year

enero	January
febrero	February
marzo	March
abril	April
mayo	May
junio	June
julio	July
agosto	August
septiembre	September
octubre	October
noviembre	November
diciembre	December

Days of the week

lunes	Monday
martes	Tuesday
miércoles	Wednesday
jueves	Thursday
viernes	Friday
sábado	Saturday
domingo	Sunday
el lunes	on Monday
los lunes	on Mondays
cada lunes	every Monday

Quantities

bastante	enough
exactamente	exactly
mucho/a/s	much, many
nada	nothing
solamente	only
suficiente	enough
un kilo de	a kilo of
un litro de	a litre of
un paquete de	a packet of
un pedazo de	a piece of
un poco de	a little of
un tarro de	a jar of
un tercio de	a third of
una botella de	a bottle of
una caja de	a box of
una docena de	a dozen
una lata de	a tin of
una parte de	a part of
una rebanada de	a slice of
varios/as	several

Continents

África (f)	Africa
América del Norte (f)	North America
América del Sur (f)	South America
Asia (f)	Asia
Australia (f)	Australia
Europa (f)	Europe

Countries

Alemania (f)	Germany
Argelia (f)	Algeria
Argentina (f)	Argentina
Austria (f)	Austria
Bélgica (f)	Belgium
Brasil (m)	Brazil
China (f)	China
Dinamarca (f)	Denmark
Egipto (m)	Egypt
Escocia (f)	Scotland
España (f)	Spain
Estados Unidos (mpl)	United States
Francia (f)	France
Gran Bretaña (f)	Great Britain
Grecia (f)	Greece
Holanda (f)	Holland
India (f)	India
Inglaterra (f)	England
Irlanda (f)	Ireland
Italia (f)	Italy
México (m)	Mexico
Nigeria (f)	Nigeria
País de Gales (m)	Wales
Países Bajos (mpl)	Netherlands
Pakistán (m)	Pakistan
Perú (m)	Peru
Reino Unido (m)	United Kingdom
Rusia (f)	Russia
Suecia (f)	Sweden
Suiza (f)	Switzerland
Tailandia (f)	Thailand
Turquía (f)	Turkey

Nationalities

alemán/ana	German
americano/a	American
argelino/a	Algerian
argentino/a	Argentinian
austríaco/a	Austrian
belga	Belgian
brasileño/a	Brazilian
británico/a	British
chino/a	Chinese
danés/esa	Danish
egipcio/a	Egyptian
escocés/esa	Scottish
español(a)	Spanish
europeo/a	European
francés/esa	French
galés/esa	Welsh
griego/a	Greek
holandés/esa	Dutch
indio/a	Indian
inglés/esa	English
irlandés/esa	Irish
italiano/a	Italian
nigeriano/a	Nigerian
mexicano/a	Mexican
pakistaní	Pakistani
ruso/a	Russian
sueco/a	Swedish
suizo/a	Swiss
tailandés/esa	Thai
turco/a	Turkish
venezolano/a	Venezuelan

Now try this

Practise the days of the week and the months of the year by talking about the birthdays of family and friends in Spanish.

109

Had a look ☐   **Nearly there** ☐   **Nailed it!** ☐

① High-frequency language

Prepositions

a	at, to
a causa de	because of
a través de	through
al final de	at the end of
al lado de	next to
alrededor de	around
antes de	before
cerca de	near
con	with
contra	against
de, desde	from
debajo de	under
delante de	in front of
dentro de	inside
después de	after
detrás de	behind
durante	during
en	in, on
en casa de	at (someone's house)
en la esquina de	on the corner of
encima de	above
enfrente de	opposite
entre	between
excepto, salvo	except
fuera de	outside
hacia	towards
hasta	until
lejos de	far from
para	for
por	through, for
según	according to
sin	without
sobre	on

delante de
in front of

detrás de
behind

al lado de
next to

entre
between

cerca de
near to

lejos de
far from

Question words

¿Adónde?
Where to?

¿Cómo?
How?

¿Cuál?
Which?

¿Cuántos/as?
How many?

¿Dónde?
Where?

¿Para qué?
What for?

¿Cuándo?
When?

¿Cuánto?
How much?

¿Por qué?
Why?

¿Qué?
What?

¿Quién?
Who?

Social conventions

¿Diga?	hello (on the telephone)
adiós	goodbye
gracias	thank you
hasta luego	see you later
hasta mañana	see you tomorrow
hasta pronto	see you soon
hola	hi, hello
muchas gracias	thank you very much
por favor	please
¡Que te diviertas!	Enjoy yourself!
¡Que lo pases bien!	Have a good time!
saludos	best wishes
¡Socorro!	Help!

Other useful expressions

¿Cómo se escribe?	How do you spell that?
aquí lo tienes	here you are
bien	OK
buena suerte	good luck
con (mucho) gusto	with pleasure
depende	it depends
en mi opinión	in my opinion
estar a punto de	to be about to
(estoy) bien	I'm fine
he tenido bastante	I've had enough
me da igual	I don't mind
mío/a	mine
no importa (nada)	it doesn't matter
normalmente	usually
otra vez	once again
¡Qué lástima!	What a shame!
¡Qué pena!	What a shame!
por supuesto	of course

Now try this

Write a question in Spanish using each of the question words on this page.

❷ Identity and culture

Eating at home and in restaurants

albaricoque (m) ciruela (f) fresa (f) frambuesa (f) limón (m) manzana (f) melocotón (m)

melón (m) naranja (f) pera (f) piña (f) plátano (m) tomate (m) uvas (f)

aceite (m)	oil
agua (f)	water
agua mineral (f) (con gas, sin gas)	mineral water (fizzy, still)
albóndiga (f)	meatball
aliño (m)	salad dressing
almuerzo (m)	lunch
arroz (m)	rice
asado (m)	roast
asado/a	cooked
atún (m)	tuna
autoservicio (m)	self-service
azúcar (m/f)	sugar
beber	to drink
bebida (f)	drink
bistec (m)	steak
bocadillo (m)	sandwich
bollería (f) / pasteles (mpl)	French pastries / cakes
brocheta (f)	kebab
¡Buen provecho!	Enjoy your meal!
cacao (m)	cocoa
café (m)	coffee
cafetera (f)	pot of coffee
caramelos (mpl)	sweets
carne (f)	meat
carne de cerdo (f)	pork
carne de vaca (f)	beef
carne fría cortada en lonchas	cold sliced meat
carne picada (f)	mince
carta (f)	menu
cebolla (f)	onion
cena (f)	evening meal
cliente/	customer

clienta (m/f)	
coliflor (f)	cauliflower
comedor (m)	dining room
comida (f)	meal, food, lunch
comida precocinada (f)	ready meal
cordero (m)	lamb
crema (f)	cream
crudo/a	raw
champiñón (m)	mushroom
chuleta (f)	chop
cuchara (f)	spoon
cucharita (f)	teaspoon
cubierto (m)	place setting (sometimes charged)
cuchillo (m)	knife
desayuno (m)	breakfast
dulce	sweet
duro/a	hard
ensalada (f)	salad
entrada (f)	starter
espaguetis (mpl)	spaghetti
especialidad (f)	speciality
filete (m)	steak
fruta (f)	fruit
galleta (f)	biscuit
golosinas (fpl)	sweets
grasa (f)	fat, grease
grasiento/a	fatty, greasy
guisante (m)	pea
hambre (f)	hunger
hamburguesa (f)	hamburger
helado (m)	ice cream

heladería (f)	ice cream parlour
huevo (m)	egg
jamón (serrano, de York) (m)	ham (cured, cooked)
judía (f)	bean
leche (f)	milk
lechuga (f)	lettuce
limonada (f)	lemonade
lleno/a	full
loncha (f)	slice
mantel (m)	table cloth
margarina (f)	margarine
menú (del día) (m)	menu (of the day)
merienda (f)	afternoon snack
mermelada (f)	jam
mesa (f)	table
mixto/a (m)	mixed
mostaza (f)	mustard
naranjada (f)	orangeade
nata (f)	cream
orgánico/a	organic
pan (m)	bread
panecillo (m)	roll
pasta (f)	pasta
pastel (m)	cake
patata (f)	potato
patatas fritas (fpl)	chips, crisps
pepino (m)	cucumber
pescado (m)	fish
picante	hot (spicy)
pimiento (m)	pepper (vegetable)
pincho moruno (m)	kebab
pizza (f)	pizza
pizzería (f)	pizza restaurant
plato (m)	plate
plato del día (m)	dish of the day

Now try this

Make a list of all the food items you really like and a list of those you don't. Write an opinion sentence for each one. Can you justify your opinions too?

Me encanta el yogur porque es muy sabroso. Odio el atún porque no como pescado.

111

② Identity and culture

plato principal (m)	main dish
pollo (m)	chicken
pomelo (m)	grapefruit
posada (f)	inn (traditional)
postre (m)	dessert
preparar	to prepare
probar	to try
propina (f)	tip
queso (m)	cheese
rábano (m)	radish
ración (f)	portion
receta (f)	recipe
refresco (m)	fizzy drink
restaurante (m)	restaurant
riquísimo/a	delicious
sabroso/a	tasty
sal (f)	salt
salado/a	salty
salchicha (f)	sausage
salón de té (m)	tea room
salsa (f)	sauce, gravy
servilleta (f)	napkin
seta (f)	mushroom
sopa (f)	soup
supermercado (m)	supermarket
tarro (m)	jar
tarta (f)	tart, cake
té (m)	tea
tenedor (m)	fork
tener hambre	to be hungry
tener sed	to be thirsty
tortilla (f)	omelette
tostada (f)	toast
vainilla (f)	vanilla
vegetariano/a	vegetarian
verduras (fpl)	vegetables
vinagre (m)	vinegar
vino (tinto, blanco) (m)	wine (red, white)
yogur (m)	yoghurt
zanahoria (f)	carrot
zumo (de fruta) (m)	(fruit) juice

Eating at home and in restaurants

ajo (m)	garlic
ahumado/a	smoked
alcachofa (f)	artichoke
aperitivo (m)	drink before a meal
apetitoso/a	appetising
al punto	medium (steak)
amargo/a	bitter
bandeja (f)	tray
bien cocido/a	well-cooked
cerveza de barril (f)	(pump) beer
espinacas (fpl)	spinach
casero/a	homemade
ganso (m)	goose
huevo frito (m)	fried egg
huevo pasado por agua (m)	boiled egg
huevos revueltos (mpl)	scrambled eggs
leche entera (f)	full fat milk
leche (semi) desnatada (f)	(semi-)skimmed milk
mariscos (mpl)	seafood
miel (f)	honey
muy hecho (m)	well done (steak)
pato (m)	duck
pavo (m)	turkey
picante (m/f)	spicy
pistacho (m)	pistachio
platillo (m)	saucer
poco hecho (m)	rare (steak)
puerros (mpl)	leeks
queso de cabra (m)	goat's cheese
salmón (m)	salmon
ternera (f)	veal
trucha (f)	trout
tisana / infusión (f)	fruit / herbal tea

Clothes and fashion

abrigo (m)	coat
algodón (m)	cotton
anillo (m)	ring
anticuado/a	old-fashioned
bañador (m)	swimming costume
barra de labios (f) / pintalabios (m)	lipstick
brazalete (m)	bracelet
botas (fpl)	boots
bragas (fpl)	pants, briefs
calzoncillos (mpl)	underpants
camisa (f)	shirt
camiseta (f)	T-shirt
camisón (m)	nightdress
cárdigan (m)	cardigan
collar (m)	necklace
corbata (f)	tie
de cuero	leather
de hilo (m)	linen
de lana	wool
de lino (m)	linen
de lunares	spotted
de rayas	striped
elegante (m/f)	smart
estilo (m)	style
gorra (m)	cap
guante (m)	glove
holgado/a	loose
jersey (m)	jumper
joyas (fpl)	jewels
joyería (f)	jeweller's
leggings (mpl)	leggings
leotardos (m)	leggings
maquillaje (m)	make-up
marca (f)	make, brand
mediano/a (f)	medium (size)
medias (fpl)	tights
número (m)	(shoe) size
pantalón (m), pantalones (mpl)	trousers
pantalón corto (m)	shorts
paraguas (m)	umbrella
pasado/a de moda	old-fashioned
pendiente (m)	earring
perfume (m)	perfume
pijama (m)	pyjamas

Now try this

Practise combining adjectives with an item of clothing – how would you translate 'a striped shirt'? You may need these in translations or role plays, so write down a list of 10 items now, then check your answers. Remember that the adjective or adjectival phrase will go after the item of clothing.

2 Identity and culture

calcetín (m)   cinturón (m)   corbata (f)

zapato (m)   sombrero (m)   bufanda (f)

Personal information, home life and relationships

abuela (f)	grandmother
abuelita (f)	granny
abuelito (m)	grandpa
abuelo (m)	grandfather
abuelos (mpl)	grandparents
adolescente (m/f)	adolescent
adulto/a (m/f)	adult
simpático	likeable
amigo/a (m/f)	friend
amigo/a por correspondencia (m/f)	penfriend
amistad (f)	friendship
apartamento (m)	apartment
apellido (m)	surname
apodo (m)	nickname
arreglado/a	neat
ático (m)	loft
atrevido/a	adventurous
autoritario/a	bossy
barba (f)	beard
barbudo	bearded
bebé (m)	baby
beso (m)	kiss
bigote (m)	moustache
bloque de pisos (m)	block of flats
boca (f)	mouth
boda (f)	wedding
butaca (f)	armchair
calvo/a (f)	bald
cara (f)	face
carácter (m)	character
casa (f)	house
casa adosada (f)	semi-detached / terraced house
casado/a	married
casamiento (m)	marriage
celebrar	to celebrate
celebridad (f)	celebrity
chica (f)	girl
chico (m)	boy
cocina (f)	kitchen
código postal (m)	postcode
comedor (m)	dining room
cuadro (m)	painting

polo (m)	polo shirt
pulsera (f)	bracelet
probador (m)	changing room
pullover (m)	jumper
reloj (m)	watch
retro	retro
ropa (f)	clothes
ropa de deporte (f)	sports kit
sostén (m)	bra
sudadera (f)	sweatshirt
suéter (m)	sweater
talla (f)	size
tatuaje (m)	tattoo
tienda de ropa (f)	clothes shop
suelto/a	loose
sujetador (m)	bra
traje (m)	suit
traje de baño (m)	swimsuit
vaqueros (mpl)	jeans
vestido (m)	dress
vestirse	to dress
vintage	vintage
zapatería (f)	shoe shop
zapatillas de deporte (fpl)	trainers

Aiming Higher

ajustado/a	tight
apretado/a	tight
bata (f)	dressing gown
caftán (m)	caftan
ceñido/a	tight
chaqueta de punto (f)	cardigan
cortarse el pelo	to have one's hair cut
de seda	silk
de terciopelo	velvet
hiyab (m)	hijab
maquillarse	to put on make-up
modelo (m/f)	model
peinarse	to comb one's hair, to have one's hair done
pintarse	to put on make-up
sombrero de paja (m)	straw hat
teñido/a	dyed
turbante (m)	turban
zapatillas (fpl)	slippers

Now try this

Look at the clothes you and your friends are wearing today. Check you can translate them all into Spanish correctly.

Had a look ☐   Nearly there ☐   Nailed it! ☐

② Identity and culture

perro (m)

conejo (m)

gato (m)

hámster (m)

pez de colores (m)

cobaya (f),
conejillo de Indias (m)

tortuga de tierra (f)

cuarto de baño (m)	bathroom	hogar (m)	home	ojos (mpl)	eyes
cumpleaños (m)	birthday	hombre (m)	man	optimista (m/f)	optimistic
de buen /	in a good /	humor (m)	mood	padre (m)	father
mal humor	bad mood	ideal (m/f)	ideal	padres (mpl)	parents
delgado/a	thin	inaguantable (mf)	unbearable	papá (m)	dad
desagradable	nasty	inteligente (m/f)	intelligent	pelearse	to fight, argue
desván (m)	loft	invitación (f)	invitation	persona (f)	person
discutir	to argue	jardín (m)	garden	persona mayor (f)	grown-up
divorciado/a	divorced	juventud (f)	youth	personalidad (f)	personality
divorciarse	to divorce	lacio/a	straight (hair)	pesimista (m/f)	pessimistic
dormitorio (m)	bedroom	liso/a	straight (hair)	piercing (m)	body piercing
edad (f)	age	llevarse bien /	to get on well /	pintura (f)	painting
egoísta (m/f)	selfish	mal con	badly with	piso (m)	flat
enamorado/a	in love	lugar de	place of birth	primo/a (m/f)	cousin
encantador(a)	charming	nacimiento (m)		prometido/a	engaged
esposa (f)	wife	lugar de	place of	razonable (m/f)	reasonable
esposo (m)	husband	residencia (m)	residence	regalo (m)	present
estudio (m)	study	madre (f)	mother	relación (f)	relationship
familia (f)	family	malo/a	naughty	reñir	to argue
famoso/a (m/f)	celebrity	mamá (f)	mum	rizado/a	curly
fastidiar	to annoy	mandón/mandona	bossy	sala (de estar) (f)	living room
fecha de	date of birth	marido (m)	husband	salón (m)	living room
nacimiento (f)		matrimonio (m)	marriage	sensibilidad (f)	feeling
flaco/a	thin	mayor	older	sentimiento (m)	feeling
gafas (fpl)	glasses	el/la mayor (mf)	the eldest	separado/a	separated
garaje (m)	garage	miembro de la	family member	silla (f)	chair
gemelo/a (m/f)	twin	familia (m)		sillón (m)	armchair
gemelos (mpl)	twins	molestar	to annoy	sin sentido del	no sense of
gente (f)	people	muebles (mpl)	furniture	humor	humour
hablador(a)	talkative	mujer (f)	woman, wife	sobrina (f)	niece
hermana (f)	sister	multicultural	multicultural	sobrino (m)	nephew
hermanastra (f)	stepsister	nacido/a	born	solo/a	alone
hermanastro (m)	stepbrother	nieto/a (m/f)	grandchild	tacaño/a	mean
hermano (m)	brother	niño/a (m/f)	child	tía (f)	aunt
hermanos (mpl)	brothers, siblings	nombre de pila (m)	first name	tío (m)	uncle, dude
guapo/a	beautiful	normal (m/f)	normal	tipo (m)	guy, bloke
hija (f)	daughter	novia (f)	girlfriend	tonto/a	silly, foolish
hijo (m)	son	novio (m)	boyfriend	vecino/a (m/f)	neighbour
hijo/a único/a	only child	nuera (f)	daughter-in-law	vida (f)	life
				yerno (m)	son-in-law

Now try this

To help you learn the vocabulary, copy out these words, classifying them in subtopics: family members, positive characteristics, negative characteristics, neutral characteristics, house and home.

2 Identity and culture

Personal information, home life and relationships

 Aiming Higher

buena acción (f)	good deed
acosar	to bully
adoptado/a	adopted
agradecer	to thank
amueblado/a	furnished
apoyar	to support
característica (f)	character trait
celoso/a	jealous
compañero/a (m/f)	classmate
comprensivo/a	understanding
compromiso (m)	engagement
conocido/a (m/f)	acquaintance
dar las gracias a	to thank
de confianza	reliable
deprimido/a	depressed
discriminación (f)	discrimination
discusión (f)	argument
engreído/a	conceited
estar en desventaja	to be disadvantaged
equilibrado/a	well-balanced
experimentar	to experience
familiar (m)	relation
fe (f)	faith (religious)
fiel	faithful
grano (m)	spot, pimple
independiente (m/f)	independent
intimidar	to bully
irritante (m/f)	annoying
leal (m/f)	loyal
madre soltera (f)	single mother
menor de edad	underage
mimado/a	spoilt
noviazgo (m)	engagement
novia (f)	fiancée, girlfriend
novio (m)	fiancé, boyfriend
padre soltero (m)	single father
pandilla (f)	gang
parecido/a	similar
pariente (m/f)	relative
pedante (m/f)	pretentious
pelea (f)	fight, argument
parecerse (a)	to resemble, look like
pretencioso/a	pretentious
racista (m/f)	racist
reunión (f)	meeting

responsable (m/f)	reliable
riña (f)	argument
sensible (m/f)	sensitive
sentido del humor (m)	sense of humour
soltero/a	single
sufrir	to suffer
tenaz (m/f)	stubborn
terco/a	stubborn

Culture, hobbies and free time

actividad (f)	activity
afición (f)	hobby
ajedrez (m)	chess
alpinismo (m)	mountaineering
Año Nuevo (m)	New Year
asistir a	to attend (match etc.)
artes marciales (mpl)	martial arts
atletismo (m)	athletics
bádminton (m)	bádminton
bailar	to dance
baile (m)	dancing, dance
balón (m)	ball
baloncesto (m)	basketball
balonmano (m)	handball
grupo (m)	band
bicicleta de montaña (f)	mountain bike
boxeo (m)	boxing
cámara (f)	camera
salto en cama elástica (f)	trampolining
campo de deportes (m)	sports ground
cantante (m/f)	singer
celebración (f)	celebration
ciclismo (m)	cycling
clásico/a	classical, classic
colección (f)	collection
coleccionar	to collect
concierto (m)	concert
concurso (m)	competition
consola de juegos (f)	games console
club (m)	club
club de jóvenes (m)	youth club
club nocturno (m)	nightclub
Cuaresma (f)	Lent
culebrón (m)	soap opera

deporte (m)	sport
deportes de alto riesgo (mpl)	extreme sports
deportes extremos (mpl)	extreme sports
día de la Madre (m)	Mother's Day
discoteca (f)	disco, nightclub
documental (m)	documentary
ejercitar(se)	to exercise
entrenar	to train
entretenimiento (m)	entertainment
Epifanía (f)	Twelfth Night, 6th January
equipo de música (m)	stereo system
equitación (f)	horse-riding
escalada (en roca) (f)	(rock) climbing
escenario (m)	stage
espectáculo (m)	show
esquí (m)	ski
esquí acuático (m)	water skiing
fanático/a de	fanatical about
felicitar	to congratulate
¡Feliz Año Nuevo!	Happy New Year!
¡Feliz cumpleaños!	Happy birthday!
fiesta (f)	party
(fisi)culturismo (m)	body building
fútbol (m)	football
gimnasia (f)	gymnastics
grupo (m)	group
hacer deporte	to do sport
hacer ejercicio	to exercise
hacer excursionismo	to ramble
hacer vela	to sail
historia de espías / de espionaje (f)	spy story
hockey (m)	hockey
jugar a los bolos	to go bowling (tenpin)
ir de caminata	to hike
ir de paseo	to go for a walk / stroll
ir de pesca	to go fishing
judo (m)	judo
juguete (m)	toy
jugador(a) (m/f)	player
juego (m)	game
kárate (m)	karate
lectura (f)	reading
libro (m)	book
lunes de Pascua (m)	Easter Monday
máquina fotográfica (f)	camera
marcar (un gol)	to score (a goal)

Now try this

To help you learn the vocabulary, make a list of the activities you enjoy doing and any that you dislike and create some opinion sentences. Remember to give reasons for these opinions!

② Identity and culture

ir en monopatín (m)	skate boarding
montañismo (m)	mountaineering
móvil (m)	mobile phone
MP3	MP3 (file)
música (f)	music
música pop (f)	pop music
música rap (f)	rap music
nadar	to swim
natación (f)	swimming
Navidad (f)	Christmas
Nochebuena (f)	Christmas Eve
novela policíaca (f)	detective / police story
noticias (fpl)	news
obra de teatro (f)	play
ocio (m)	free time, leisure
orquesta (f)	orchestra
parapente (m)	paragliding
participar en	to participate in, to take part in
pasatiempo (m)	hobby
Pascua (f)	Easter
patinaje (m)	skating
patinar sobre ruedas	to roller-skate
película de aventuras (f)	adventure film
película de ciencia ficción (f)	science fiction film
película del Oeste (f)	Western (film)
película de fantasía (f)	fantasy film
película de terror (f)	horror film
película de misterio / suspense (f)	thriller (film)
película romántica / de amor (f)	romantic film
pelota (f)	ball
pescar	to fish
petanca (f)	boules, petanque (similar to bowls)

ping-pong (m)	table tennis
piragüismo (m)	canoeing
placer (m)	pleasure
programa de televisión (m)	TV programme
revista (f)	magazine
rugby (m)	rugby
romántico/a	romantic
sacar a pasear (al perro)	to take (the dog) for a walk
salón (m)	lounge
salto con paracaídas (m)	parachuting
ser miembro de	to be a member of
serie (f)	series
squash (m)	squash
surf/surfing (m)	surfing
tebeo (m)	comic
teclado (m)	keyboard
telenovela (f)	soap opera
tenis (m)	tennis
tenis de mesa (m)	table tennis
tiempo libre (m)	free time
vela (f)	sailing
videojuego (m)	video game
Viernes Santo (m)	Good Friday
voleibol (m)	volleyball

Culture, hobbies and free time

 Aiming Higher

equipamiento deportivo (m)	sports equipment
audiencia (f)	audience
auriculares (mpl)	earphones
barco de vela (m)	sailing boat
bricolaje (m)	DIY
campeonato (m)	championship
caña de pescar (f)	fishing rod
comedia (f)	comedy
comedia musical (f)	musical comedy, musical
conocimiento (m)	knowledge
descanso (m)	half-time
división (f)	division (sports)
drama (m)	drama
esgrima (f)	fencing
juego de mesa (m)	board game
juego electrónico (m)	electronic game
liga (f)	league
mando a distancia (m)	remote control
medio tiempo (m)	half-time
melodía (f)	melody, tune

Toco (el / la) …   I play (the) …

violín (m)	guitarra (f)	trompeta (f)	flauta (f)

clarinete (m)	piano (m)	banjo (m)	batería (f)

teclado (m)	keyboard
sitar (m)	sitar

Now try this

Write a list of the things you do in your free time and what your family members or friends do. For example:
Yo veo películas de terror y escucho música pop. Mi padre lee novelas policíacas.

② Identity and culture

película doblada (f) dubbed film
película policíaca (f) detective /
                    police film
remo (m) rowing
subtítulos (mpl) subtitles
telespectador(a) viewer
  (m/f)
televisión por cable TV
  cable (f)
televisión por satellite TV
  satélite (f)
tiro con arco (m) archery
torneo (m) tournament
velero (m) sailing boat
versión original original version
  (subtitulada) (f) (subtitled)
vestuarios (mpl) changing rooms
videocámara (f) video camera

Internet and social media

acoso cyber bullying
  cibernético (m)
almacenar to store
archivar to save
barra oblicua (f) forward slash
blog (m) blog
borrar to erase, delete
cámara web (f) webcam
cargar to load, upload
charlar en línea to chat online
chat (m) chatroom
chatear to chat (online)
conexión (f) connection
contraseña (de password
  acceso) (f)
correo email
  electrónico (m)
descargar to download
digital digital
disco (m) disk
email (m) email
escribir a to type
  ordenador
grabar to burn, record
guardar to store
impresora (f) printer
imprimir to print
Internet (m) internet
ordenador (m) computer
página de internet page
  Internet (f)

página de inicio (f) homepage
página frontal (f) homepage
página web (f) webpage
pantalla (f) screen
programador(a) programmer
  (m/f)
quemar to burn
ratón (m) mouse
red social (f) social network
riesgo (m) risk
seguridad (f) security
software (m) software
sondeo (m) survey
subir to upload
tecla (f) key (on keyboard)
teclado (m) keyboard
virus (m) virus
webcam (f) webcam
website (m) website

Aiming Higher

archivo de data file
  datos (m)
arroba (f) @ (at)
base de datos (m) database
correo web (m) webmail
disco duro (m) hard disk
enlace (m) link
pantalla táctil (f) touchscreen
procesador de word processor
  texto (m)
subrayar to underscore
tarjeta de memory card
  memoria (f)

Now try this

Translate the following into Spanish:
1 I like to chat online with my friends in the evening.
2 Cyber bullying is not a problem at my school.
3 I want to be a programmer when I leave school.

③ Local area, holiday and travel

al / en el norte
in the north

al / en el oeste   al / en el este
in the west   in the east

al / en el sur
in the south

El castillo está en el norte de la ciudad.

Visitor information

¡Que lo pases bien! Enjoy your stay!
abierto/a — open
acera (f) — pavement
afueras (fpl) — outskirts
al aire libre — in the open air
al extranjero — abroad
aldea (f) — small village
alquilar — to rent
alquiler de coches / car / bike hire
  bicicletas (m)
anuncio (m) — advertisement
apartamento (m) — apartment
autopista (f) — motorway
barrio (m) — part of town
bienvenido/a — welcome
bosque (m) — wood
cafetería (f) — café
caja (f) — till, cash desk
campo (m) — field,
  countryside
capital (f) — capital city
carnet de — identity card
  identidad (m)
cartel (m) — poster
castillo (m) — castle
catedral (f) — cathedral
centro de la — town centre
  ciudad (m)

cerrado/a — closed
cerveza de barril (f) — draught beer
cita (f) — appointment
ciudad (f) — city
colina (f) — hill
comunidad — autonomous
  autónoma (f) — community
concierto (m) — concert
control de — passport
  pasaportes (m) — control
costa (f) — coast
descuento (m) — reduction
día de fiesta (m) — public holiday
entrada (f) — entrance,
  admission
entretenimiento (m) — entertainment
escaparate (m) — shop window
estar situado/a — to be situated
excursión (f) — tour
exposición (f) — exhibition
extranjero/a (m/f) — foreigner
fiesta (f) — festival
fiesta nacional (f) — public holiday
folleto (m) — brochure / leaflet
fuera — outside
habitante (m/f) — inhabitant
histórico/a — historic
horario de — opening hours
  apertura (m)
industrial (m/f) — industrial
isla (f) — island
lago (m) — lake

lista de precios (f) — price list
lugar de interés (m) — place of interest
mapa de — road map
  carreteras (m)
mar (m) — sea
medios de — media
  comunicación (mpl)
mercado (m) — market
montaña (f) — mountain
monumento (m) — monument
naturaleza (f) — nature
ocio (m) — leisure
oficina de turismo — tourist office
oficina de — tourist
  información — information
  turística — office
país (m) — country
parque de — amusement
  atracciones (m) — park
parte (f) — part (of town)
peatón/ona (m/f) — pedestrian
película (f) — film
periódico (m) — newspaper
pintoresco/a — picturesque
piso (m) — flat
plano (m) — map
playa (f) — beach
plaza (f) — square
polución (f) — pollution
postal (f) — postcard
póster (m) — poster
precio de — entry fee
  entrada (m)

Now try this

Pick out 10–15 words from this page that you could use to describe a recent trip or holiday. Memorise them, then try to write a short sentence with each.

③ Local area, holiday and travel

prensa (f)	press	memoria (f)	memory	frutería (f)	fruit shop
prohibido/a	forbidden	rastro (m)	fleamarket	galería de arte (f)	art gallery
provincia (f)	province	recuerdo (m)	souvenir	gasolinera (f)	petrol station
público/a	public	salida de	emergency exit	grandes	department
pueblo (m)	town	emergencia (f)		almacenes (mpl)	store
recorrido (m)	tour	suceso (m)	event	granja (f)	farm
recuerdo (m)	souvenir	tener lugar	to take place	hospital (m)	hospital
región (f)	region	vacaciones de	skiing holiday	iglesia (f)	church
reservar	to book	esquí (fpl)		industria (f)	industry
río (m)	river	vacaciones de	winter holiday	lavandería	laundry
salida (f)	exit	invierno (fpl)		(automática) (f)	(launderette)
selva tropical (f)	rainforest	viaje organizado (m)	package holiday	librería (f)	book shop
señal (f)	sign			mercado (m)	market
sitio (m)	place	**Facilities**		municipal (m/f)	public, municipal
suburbio (m)	suburb	abierto/a	open	museo (m)	museum
tarjeta	telephone card	aeropuerto (m)	airport	negocio (m)	business
telefónica (f)		aseos (mpl)	toilets	oficina de	post office
torre (f)	tower	ayuntamiento (m)	town hall	correos (f)	
tranquilo/a	quiet	banco (m)	bank	palacio (m)	palace
turista (m/f)	tourist	banco (m)	seat, bench	parque (m)	park
vale la pena ver	well worth	biblioteca (f)	library	patio (de	playground
	seeing	bloque de pisos (m)	tower block	recreo) (m)	
vida nocturna (f)	nightlife	bolera (f)	bowling alley	pescadería (f)	fishmonger's
visita (f)	visit		(tenpin)	piscina (cubierta) (f)	(indoor) pool
visita guiada a	walking tour	café (m)	café	pista de (patinaje	ice rink
pie (f)		cafetería (f)	café	sobre) hielo (f)	
zona (f)	part of town	cancha de tenis (f)	tennis court	policía (m/f)	police officer
zona peatonal (f)	pedestrian area	carnicería (f)	butcher's	policía (mf)	policeman/
zona	suburb	castillo (m)	castle	guardia civil (m/f)	woman
residencial (f)		catedral (f)	cathedral	polideportivo (m)	leisure centre
zona verde (f)	park, green	centro	shopping centre	puente (m)	bridge
	space	comercial (m)		puerto (m)	port
		centro de ocio (m)	leisure centre	quiosco (m)	newspaper stall
Visitor information		cerrado/a	closed	servicios (mpl)	toilets
		cine (m)	cinema	supermercado (m)	supermarket
Aiming Higher		clínica (f)	hospital, clinic	teatro (m)	theatre
		club nocturno (m)	nightclub	tienda (f)	shop
acontecimiento (m)	event	comercio (m)	business	tienda de	grocer's
aduana (f)	customs	comisaría (f)	police station	comestibles (f)	
alrededores (mpl)	surrounding area	Correos (m)	Post Office		
canal (m)	canal	cubo de basura (m)	rubbish bin	**Aiming Higher**	
centro turístico	seaside resort	discoteca (f)	disco, nightclub		
costero (m)		edificio (m)	building	caja de ahorros (f)	savings bank
centro de la	town centre	estación de	bus station	cajero	cashpoint, ATM
ciudad (m)		autobuses (f)		automático (m)	
desfile (m)	procession	estación de	railway station	ferretería (f)	hardware shop
estancia (f)	stay	ferrocarril (f)		limpieza en seco (f)	dry cleaning
experiencia (f)	experience	estación de	service station	parque zoológico /	zoo
fuegos	fireworks	servicio (f)		zoo (m)	
artificiales (mpl)		estadio (m)	stadium	tintorería (f)	dry cleaner's
fuente (f)	fountain	fábrica (f)	factory	torre de pisos (m)	tower block
hospitalidad (f)	hospitality	farmacia (f)	chemist's		

Now try this

Think about a place you have been on holiday or somewhere you would like to go. Make a list of the facilities and types of accommodation it has.

119

Had a look ☐   **Nearly there** ☐   **Nailed it!** ☐

3 Local area, holiday and travel

Accommodation

acampar	to camp
agua potable (f)	drinking water
albergue juvenil (m)	youth hostel
alojamiento (m)	accommodation
alquería (f)	farm house
alquilar	to hire, rent
almohada (f)	pillow
amueblado/a	furnished
apagar	to turn / switch off
armario (m)	wardrobe
ascensor (m)	lift
balcón (m)	balcony
bañera (f)	bath tub
baño (m)	bathroom
calefacción (f)	heating
cama (f)	bed
camping (m)	campsite
caravana (f)	caravan
cepillo de dientes (m)	toothbrush
colonia de vacaciones (f)	holiday camp
colonia de verano (f)	summer camp
cuarto de baño (m)	bathroom
deshacer la maleta	to unpack
ducha (f)	shower
dueño/a (m/f)	owner
en el campo	in the country
en el primer piso	on the first floor
encender	to turn / switch on
equipaje (m)	luggage
escalera (f)	staircase
formulario (f)	form
funcionar	to work
garaje (m)	garage
habitación de dos camas (f)	twin room
habitación doble (f)	double room
habitación individual (f)	single room
hotel (m)	hotel
incluido/a	included
jabón (m)	soap

jardín (m)	garden
lavabo (m)	wash basin
libre	vacant
litera (f)	bunk bed
llave (f)	key
llegada (f)	arrival
maleta (f)	suitcase
media pensión (f)	half-board
ocupado/a	occupied
papel higiénico (m)	toilet paper
pasta de dientes (f)	toothpaste
pensión (f)	guest house
pensión completa (f)	full board
piso (m)	floor, flat
planta (f)	floor
planta baja (f)	ground floor
puerta (principal) (f)	(front) door
recepción (f)	reception
recepcionista (m/f)	receptionist
ropa de cama (f)	bed linen
sábana (f)	sheet
saco de dormir (m)	sleeping bag
sala de juegos (f)	games room
salida (f)	exit
salón (m)	lounge
segundo/a	second
sótano (m)	basement
suelo (m)	floor
suplemento (m)	supplement
tienda (de campaña) (f)	tent
toalla de baño (f)	bath towel
ventana (f)	window
vista (f)	view

Aiming Higher

aire acondicionado (m)	air conditioning
alojamiento (m)	accomodation
alojarse	to stay
confirmar	to confirm
registro (f)	registration / booking in
ruido (m)	noise
salida de emergencia (f)	emergency exit

Transport

a pie	on foot
aeropuerto (m)	airport
andén (m)	platform
aparcamiento (m)	car park
asiento (m)	seat
atasco (m)	traffic jam
autobús (m)	bus
autocar (m)	coach
autopista (f)	motorway
autovía (f)	main road
avión (m)	plane
barco (m)	boat
bici (f)	bike
billete (m)	ticket
calle (f)	street
camino (m)	way, road
camión (m)	lorry
carretera (f)	road
ciclomotor (m)	moped
circulación (f)	traffic
coche (m)	car
coche-cama (m)	sleeping car
compartimento (m)	compartment
conductor(a) (m/f)	driver
conexión (f)	connection
consigna (f)	left luggage
cruce (m)	crossroads
de ida	single
de ida y vuelta	return
de segunda clase	second class
descuento (f)	reduction
despegar	to take off (plane)
desvío (m)	detour
dirección (f)	direction
dirección única (f)	one-way street
directo/a	direct
enlace (m)	connection
estación de autobuses (f)	bus / coach station
ferry (m)	ferry
gasoil (m)	diesel
gasolina (f)	petrol
glorieta (f)	roundabout
horario (m)	timetable
línea (f)	line / route

Now try this

Imagine you go on holiday and travel somewhere on public transport, but it is the journey from hell! Write some sentences to describe what happened.

Had a look ☐   Nearly there ☐   Nailed it! ☐

Vocabulary

③ Local area, holiday and travel

medio de transporte (m)	means of transport
mostrador de billetes (m)	ticket office
moto (f)	motorbike
ocupado/a	occupied / taken
parada (f)	bus stop
pasajero/a	passenger
paso de peatones (m)	pedestrian crossing
perder	to miss (train, etc.)
permiso de conducir (m)	driving licence
por adelantado	in advance
prioridad (a la derecha) (f)	priority (to the right)
puerto (m)	port
retraso (m)	delay
revisor(a) (m/f)	ticket inspector
sala de espera (f)	waiting room
salida (f)	departure, exit
semáforo (mpl)	traffic lights
señal (f)	sign
sentido (m)	direction
sentido único (m)	one-way system
sin plomo	unleaded
taxi (m)	taxi
tranvía (f)	tram
tren (m)	train
validar	to validate (a ticket)
ventanilla de billetes (f)	ticket office
vía (f)	platform, track
viaje (m)	journey

Aiming Higher

adelantar	to overtake
atropellar	to run over
cinturón de seguridad (m)	seatbelt
embarcar	to board, embark

frenar	to brake
helicóptero (m)	helicopter
hora punta (f)	rush hour
límite de velocidad (m)	speed limit
pasaje a nivel (m)	level crossing
peaje (m)	toll
prohibido aparcar	no parking
salida de autopista (f)	motorway junction
salida de emergencia (f)	emergency exit
vehículo de gran tonelaje (m)	heavy goods vehicle

Directions

a la derecha	on the right
a la izquierda	on the left
atravesar	to cross
de cerca	near
cruzar	to cross
doblar	to turn
está a 100 metros	it's 100 metres away
estar situado/a	to be situated
esquina (f)	corner
hasta	as far as
la primera a la derecha	the first on the right
la segunda a la izquierda	the second on the left
lejos	far
seguir todo recto	to go straight on
tomar	to take

Holiday problems

accidente (m)	accident
asegurar	to insure
avería (f)	breakdown
billetero (m)	wallet
cambiar	to exchange, replace
cantidad (f)	quantity
cartera (f)	wallet
colisión (f)	collision
daño (m)	damage
defecto (m)	fault
descuento (m)	reduction, discount
devolver	to give back
dirección (f)	address
entrega (f)	delivery
entregar	to deliver
error (m)	mistake
factura (f)	bill
formulario (m)	form
garantía (f)	guarantee
garantizar	to guarantee
hacer reparto(s)	to deliver
(servicio de) información y reclamaciones	customer service
monedero (m)	purse
piezas de recambio (fpl)	replacement parts
pagar	to pay
queja (f)	complaint
quejarse	to complain
rebaja (f)	reduction
recibo (m)	receipt
reemplazar	to replace
reparar	to repair
robo (m)	theft
roto/a	broken
seguro (m)	insurance
volver	to return

Now try this

Choose two places you know well which you can walk or drive to in 5–10 minutes. Now describe the route in Spanish. Make sure you include as many details as possible to make it easy for someone to follow. Use the following instructions: 'toma' for 'take', 'dobla' for 'turn' and 'cruza' for 'cross'.

121

❸ Local area, holiday and travel

Weather

hace sol

hace frío

hace calor

hace viento

hay tormenta

está nublado

llueve

nieva

boletín meteorológico (m)	weather report	lluvioso/a	rainy	medio/a	average
		mal tiempo (m)	bad weather	mejorar	to brighten up
brillar	to shine	nevar	to snow	período soleado (m)	bright spell
buen tiempo (m)	good weather	nieva, está nevando	it is snowing		
calor (m)	heat			precipitación (f)	rainfall
caluroso/a	hot	nieve (f)	snow	pronóstico meteorológico (m)	weather forecast
cambiar	to change	nube (f)	cloud		
cielo (m)	sky	seco/a	dry		
clima (m)	climate	sol (m)	sun	temperatura media (f)	average temperature
estación (f)	season	soleado/a	sunny		
está helado	it is freezing	temperatura más alta (f)	highest temperature	tormentoso/a	stormy
está nublado	it's overcast			variable (m/f)	changeable
frío (m)	cold	tiempo (m)	weather		
grado (m)	degree (temperature)	tormenta (f)	storm		
		viento (m)	wind		

hace mucho frío — it's freezing
hay niebla — it's foggy
hay relámpagos — there's lightning
hay truenos — there's thunder
helada (f) — frost
helar — to freeze
llover — to rain
llueve, está lloviendo — it's raining
lluvia (f) — rain

Aiming Higher

alto/a — high
bajo/a — low
despejarse — to brighten up
granizar — to hail
granizo (m) — hail
hay neblina — it is misty

Now try this

Close your book and write down as many weather expressions as you can in one minute. Then check here to see which ones you did not remember.

④ School

adecuado/a	satisfactory
alemán (m)	German
alumno/a (m/f)	student
año escolar / académico (m)	school year
aprobar (un examen)	to pass (an exam)
árabe (m)	Arabic
arte (m)	art
arte dramático (m)	drama
asignatura (f)	subject
aula (f)	classroom
ausente	absent
autobús escolar (m)	school bus
bachillerato (m)	equivalent of A levels
biblioteca (f)	library
biología (f)	biology
bloc de notas (m)	pad of paper
boletín de notas (m)	school report
bolígrafo, boli (m)	ballpoint pen
calculadora (f)	calculator
calificación (f)	mark
campo de deportes (m)	sports field
cantina (f)	canteen
cartera (f)	school bag
castigo (m)	detention
ciclomotor (m)	moped
ciencias (fpl)	sciences
clase (f)	classroom, lesson
cocina (f)	food technology
colegio privado (m)	private school
conserje (m/f)	caretaker
contestar	to answer
continuar con	to continue with
copiar	to copy
corbata (f)	tie
coro (m)	choir
corregir	to correct
cuaderno (m)	exercise book
deberes (mpl)	homework
débil	unsatisfactory
desarrollo (m)	progress
descanso para comer (m)	lunch break
despacho (m)	office
dibujo (m)	art
diccionario (m)	dictionary
director(a) (m/f)	headteacher
discutir	to discuss
diseño (m)	DT
durar	to last
educación física (f)	PE
educación personal, social y sanitaria (f)	PSE, PSHE
Educación Secundaria Obligatoria (f)	GCSE equivalent
ejercicio (m)	exercise
enseñar	to teach
equipo (m)	team
escrito/a	written
escuela de educación primaria (f)	primary school
escuela pública (f)	state school
español (m)	Spanish
estado (m)	state
estricto/a	strict
estuche (m)	pencil case
estudiante (m/f)	student
estudiar	to study
evaluación (f)	test
examen (m)	exam
excursión del instituto (f)	school trip
éxito (m)	success
experimento (m)	experiment
física (f)	physics
flojo/a en	weak, bad at (subject)
francés (m)	French
fuerte en (m/f)	good at (subject)
geografía (f)	geography
gimnasia (f)	gymnastics
gimnasio (m)	gym
goma (f)	rubber
hacer un examen	to sit an exam
historia (f)	history
hoja de ejercicios (f)	worksheet
hoja de examen (f)	exam paper
horario (m)	timetable
humanidades (fpl)	humanities
idioma (m)	foreign (language)
inadecuado/a	inadequate
informática (f)	ICT
inglés (m)	English
injusto/a	unfair
instituto de educacíon secundaria (m)	secondary school
instituto para alumnos de 16 a 18 años (m)	sixth form college
intercambio (m)	exchange
italiano (m)	Italian
japonés (m)	Japanese
jornada escolar (f)	school day
justo/a	fair
laboratorio (m)	laboratory
laboratorio de idiomas (m)	language lab
lápiz (m)	pencil
latín (m)	Latin
lengua (f)	language
lenguas extranjeras (f)	foreign languages
libro de texto escolar (m)	school book
listo/a	clever
mandarín (m)	Mandarin
matemáticas (fpl)	maths
materia (f)	school subject
mixto/a	mixed
música (f)	music
muy buena nota (f)	very good mark
norma (f)	rule
orientador(a) (m/f)	careers adviser
orientación profesional (f)	careers advice
página (f)	page
parvulario (m)	nursery school
pasillo (m)	corridor
patio de recreo (m)	playground
pegamento (m)	glue
perezoso/a	lazy
periódico del instituto (m)	school newspaper
periodismo (m)	media studies, journalism
pizarra (f)	board
planes para el futuro (mpl)	future plans
pluma (estilográfica) (f)	(fountain) pen
polideportivo (m)	sports hall
práctica (f)	exercise
practicar	to practise
pregunta (f)	question
preescolar (m)	pre-school
prestar atención	to pay attention
progreso (m)	progress
proyector (m)	projector
prueba (f)	class test
pupitre (m)	desk
química (f)	chemistry
(re)llenar	to fill out
recreo (m)	break time
regla (f)	ruler
religión (f)	RE, religion
rendimiento (m)	success
repasar	to revise
reportaje (m)	report
respuesta (f)	answer
reunión (f)	assembly
rotulador (m)	felt-tip pen

Now try this

Can you list all the subjects you are studying and spell them correctly? Can you also write down the facilities that your school has?

④ School

sacapuntas (m)	sharpener
sala de profesores (f)	staff room
seguir	to continue
semestre (m)	semester
sociología (f)	sociology
suspender (un examen)	to fail (an exam)
tarea (f)	task
tecnología (f)	technology
tecnología de alimentos (f)	food technology
tecnología del diseño (f)	DT
tener cuidado	to be careful
tijeras (fpl)	scissors
título (m)	qualification
trabajador/a (m/f)	hardworking
trimestre (m)	term
uniforme (m)	uniform
universidad (f)	university
vacaciones de mitad de trimestre (fpl)	half-term
vacaciones de verano (fpl)	summer holidays
sala de actos del colegio/del instituto (f)	school hall
vestuario (m)	changing room
vuelta al instituto (m)	first day back at school

Aiming Higher

a distancia	distance (learning)
auriculares (mpl)	headphones
auxiliar de lengua (m/f)	foreign language assistant
cartucho de tinta (m)	ink cartridge
centro de capacitación (m)	training centre
conocimiento (m)	knowledge
dejar	to drop (a subject)
deletrear	to spell
derecho (m)	law
dotado/a	gifted
economía (f)	economics
estar castigado/a	to have a detention
estar de acuerdo con	to agree with
estudios (mpl)	studies
examen de fin de curso (m)	end of year exam
explicar	to explain
habilidades (fpl)	skills
hacer novillos	to play truant
internado (m)	boarding school
hacer un castigo escrito	to do a written punishment, lines

lector(a) (m/f)	foreign language assistant
libro de texto (m)	text book
licenciatura (f)	degree (university)
mejorar	to improve
optativo/a	optional
pasar lista (f)	to take the register
pasar de curso	to move up (a year)
pérdida de tiempo (f)	waste of time
permiso (m)	permission
presión (f)	pressure (to do well)
pronunciación (f)	pronunciation
reunión (de padres) (f)	(parents') meeting
se ha cancelado	has been cancelled
título (m)	degree (university)
trabajo (m)	essay
traducción (f)	translation

Now try this

List three things you plan to do after your exams and explain why you want to do them. Then write three sentences about things you won't do and why.

❺ Future aspirations, study and work

actor (m/f)	actor
agencia de viajes (f)	travel agency
agente de policía (m/f)	police officer
agricultor(a) (m/f)	farmer
albañil (m)	builder
ambición (f)	ambition
anuncio (m)	advertisment
archivo (m)	file
archivar	to file
arquitecto/a (m/f)	architect
artista (m/f)	artist
azafato/a (m/f)	air steward(ess)
beneficiencia (f)	charity
bien pagado/a	well paid
cajero/a (m/f)	cashier
camarero/a (m/f)	waiter / waitress
carnicero/a (m/f)	butcher
carpeta (f)	folder
cocinero/a (m/f)	chef
colega (m/f)	colleague
colgar	to hang up
comercio (m)	business
como voluntario/a (m/f)	as a volunteer
compañía (f)	company
concurrido/a	busy
condiciones de empleo (mpl)	terms of employment
conductor(a) (m/f)	driver
con experiencia	with experience
conferencia (f)	conference
contestador automático (m)	answering machine
costura (f)	sewing
dentista (m/f)	dentist
desempleado/a	unemployed
director(a) (m/f)	manager
diseñador(a) (m/f)	designer
educativo/a	educational
electricista (m/f)	electrician
empleado/a (m/f)	employee
empleo (m)	job
empresa (f)	company
empresario/a (m/f)	employer
en el extranjero	abroad
enfermero/a (m/f)	nurse
entrevista de trabajo (f)	job interview
esfuerzo (m)	work, effort
estudiante (m/f)	student
expediente (m)	file
experiencia laboral (f)	work experience
farmacéutico/a (m/f)	pharmacist
fontanero/a (m/f)	plumber
formación (f)	training
funcionario/a (m/f)	civil servant
granjero/a (m/f)	farmer
hacer un curso	to do a course
informático/a (m/f)	computer scientist
ingeniero/a (m/f)	engineer
formacíon profesional (f)	training
lenguaje (m)	language
llamada telefónica (f)	telephone call
mal pagado/a	badly paid
marcar el número	to dial the number
mecánico/a (m/f)	mechanic
médico/a (m/f)	doctor
mensaje (m)	message
mercadotecnia (f)	marketing
moda (f)	fashion
músico/a (m/f)	musician
negocio (m)	business
ocupado/a	busy
panadero/a	baker
pastelero/a	baker, cake maker
periodista (m/f)	journalist
planificado/a	planned
poeta (m/f)	poet
por hora	per hour
prácticas profesionales (m)	apprenticeship
profesor(a) (m/f)	teacher
programador(a) (m/f)	programmer
rellenar un formulario	to fill in a form
representante de ventas (m/f)	sales rep
reunión (f)	meeting
salario (m)	salary
sastrería (f)	tailoring
sin cobrar	without pay
solicitar un trabajo	to apply for a job
sueldo (m)	salary
sueño (m)	dream
técnico/a (m/f)	technician
a tiempo parcial	part time
tienda (f)	shop
trabajador(a) agrícola (m/f)	farmworker
trabajo (m)	job
una organización benéfica (f)	to work for a charity
universidad (f)	university
voluntariamente	voluntarily

Aiming Higher

en beneficio de	in aid of
adjuntar	to enclose
adjunto/a	enclosed, attached
aprendiz (m/f)	apprentice
aprendizaje (m)	apprenticeship
ascenso (m)	promotion
titulado	qualified
carta de solicitud (f)	letter of application
cita (f)	appointment
enseñanza superior (f)	higher education
enviar	to send
firma (f)	signature
impresión (f)	impression
incluir	to enclose
inscribirse	to enrol, apply
prácticas profesionales (m)	internship
ley (f)	law
mandar	to send
matricularse	to enrol
medicina (f)	medicine
meta (f)	goal
objetivo (m)	objective
ocupación (f)	occupation
oficio (m)	job
posibilidades de promoción (fpl)	promotion prospects
posición (f)	position
presentarse	to introduce oneself
profesión (f)	profession
propósito (m)	aim
rellenar	to fill in
solicitar en	to apply at
solicitar un puesto de trabajo	to apply for a job
solicitud (f)	application form
titulado/a	qualified
título (m)	qualification
vacante (m)	vacancy
venta benéfica (f)	charity sale

Now try this

Write down a list of four people in your family or friends who work.

Now write down notes in Spanish, next to their names:

· What job they do

· Whether they like it and why

Finally write a sentence in Spanish from your notes about each person.

Had a look ☐　**Nearly there** ☐　**Nailed it!** ☐

6 International and global dimension

agua potable (f)	drinking water
medio ambiente (m)	environment
animales (mpl)	animals
basura (f)	rubbish
beneficiencia (f)	charity
campaña (f)	campaign
campo (m)	country(side)
carbón (m)	coal
comercio justo (m)	fair trade
contaminación (f)	pollution
contra	against
desastre (m)	disaster
desventajas (fpl)	disadvantages
electricidad (f)	electricity
energía (f)	energy, power
falta (de) (f)	lack (of)
gas (m)	gas
gente (f)	people
global (m/f)	global
guerra (f)	war
hambre (f)	hunger
huracán (m)	hurricane
internacional (m/f)	international
inundaciones (fpl)	flooding, floods
Juegos Olímpicos (mpl)	Olympic Games
mundial (m)	world cup (football)
mundo (m)	world
morir	to die
país (m)	country
petróleo (m)	oil
planeta (m)	planet
pobreza (f)	poverty
polución (f)	pollution
por	for
protección (f)	protection
proteger	to protect
reciclaje (m)	recycling
reciclar	to recycle
recursos naturales (mpl)	natural resources
selva tropical (f)	rainforest
sequía (f)	drought
tierra (f)	earth
ventaja (f)	advantage
vivir	to live

Aiming Higher

agua dulce (f)	freshwater
agua salada (f)	saltwater
amenazar	to threaten
aprovechar	to benefit (from)
calentamiento global (m)	global warming
climático/a	climatic
contaminar	to contaminate, pollute
convertir en abono	to (make into) compost
cuidar	to save, keep safe
derechos (mpl)	rights
necesitado/a	unfortunate, needy
energía solar (f)	solar power
especie (m)	species
espiando	spying
faltar	to be lacking
inmediato/a	instant
mantener el contacto	to stay in contact
seguridad (f)	security
separar	to sort / separate
sobrevivir	to survive
terremoto (m)	earthquake
volcán (m)	volcano

Now try this

Close this book. Design a poster to show the issues currently facing our world. Label it in Spanish and then check that your poster has the correct vocabulary and spellings.

Answers

Identity and culture

1. Physical descriptions

(a) Antonio, (b) Ana, (c) Pedro, (d) Elena, (e) Antonio

2. Character descriptions

Listen to the recording · SPEAKING TRACK 47

Sample answer

En mi opinión, soy bastante equilibrado y creo que también soy muy razonable. No obstante, no estoy muy seguro de mí mismo y puedo ser un poco tímido. Cuando era pequeño, era muy travieso y un poco tacaño con mis hermanos.

3. Describing family

B

4. Friends

Listen to the recording · SPEAKING TRACK 48

Sample answer

En mi opinión, los amigos están ahí para apoyarte; no siempre están a tu lado, pero pueden guardar tus secretos. Deben aceptarte como eres. Creo que los amigos son tan importantes como la familia. Es esencial que los amigos se lleven bien. A mi parecer, la amistad es más importante que el amor.

6. Relationships

Sample answer

Me llevo bien con la mayoría de mis compañeros del cole porque son simpáticos y amables, pero discutimos de vez en cuando. Los profes son comprensivos y trabajadores, entonces los respeto. Hace unos días, un alumno robó el móvil de mi amigo y sus padres se quejaron a la directora, pero afortunadamente, los problemas de robos son raros porque las relaciones entre los alumnos y los profes son buenas. El año que viene, me quedaré en el mismo cole porque tengo muchos amigos aquí.

7. When I was younger

(a) They used to climb big trees in the garden.
(b) They used to watch their favourite programmes on TV.

8. Peer group pressure

Sample answer

Mi amiga Laura tiene gafas y es bastante alta. Es una chica muy inteligente pero a veces es un poco tímida. Para mí una buena amiga debe guardar los secretos y decir la verdad. Gracias a ella empecé a comer de un modo más sano y no cedí ante la presión del grupo para beber alcohol o para tomar malas decisiones. En el futuro, Laura y yo vamos a hacer más deporte. Me gustaría aprender a montar a caballo.

9. Customs

(i) in big cities
(ii) that the siesta increases productivity

10. Everyday life

Sample answer

Normalmente me levanto a las seis y media y me ducho rápido. Luego desayuno cereales y voy al instituto a pie. El fin de semana pasado me levanté muy tarde porque estaba bastante cansado después de jugar al fútbol el viernes por la noche. Durante tu visita podemos ver algunos monumentos famosos de Londres y durante el fin de semana vamos a ver un partido de fútbol en el estadio cerca de mi casa. El domingo mis amigos van a ir a una fiesta y si quieres podemos ir con ellos.

11. Meals at home

(a) it tastes better
(b) by being organised
(c) to be interested in the rest of the family

12. Food and drink

Listen to the recording · SPEAKING TRACK 49

Sample answer

C = candidate, T = teacher
T: Usted está en un restaurante de España.
T: ¿En qué puedo servirle?
C: Quiero una mesa para cuatro personas, por favor.
T: Muy bien. ¿Qué quiere comer?
C: Me gustaría la tortilla de patatas y una ensalada mixta.
T: Perfecto. ¿Y para beber?
C: Me gustaría tomar agua mineral.
T: ¿La comida está bien?
C: Sí, me gusta mucho la tortilla. Es deliciosa.
T: Muy bien. ¿Tiene una pregunta?
C: ¿Cuánto es en total?
T: Son treinta y ocho euros.

13. Shopping for clothes

A

14. Social media

B

15. Technology

(a) Nuria, (b) Gabriela, (c) Mateo, (d) Pablo, (e) Nuria

16. The internet

Sample answer

Normalmente compro por Internet porque es barato y bastante fácil. En casa, mis padres suelen enviar y recibir correos electrónicos pero mi hermana y yo leemos páginas web y utilizamos los chats. El año pasado me compré un móvil nuevo por Internet. Hoy estoy navegando por Internet para buscar unos auriculares.

17. Pros and cons of technology

B, C, F

18. Hobbies

A loves reading [Teresa]
B goes shopping with friends [Leonardo]
D goes swimming every day [Carmen]

19. Music

Sample answer

A mí me encanta la música y ahora estoy aprendiendo a tocar la guitarra. Antes tocaba el teclado pero después de ir a un concierto de un guitarrista muy bueno, decidí aprender a tocar la guitarra. Es un instrumento que tiene un sonido suave y bonito. En el futuro tengo la intención de tocar en un grupo con unos amigos del instituto porque me encanta participar en conciertos con otra gente.

20. Sport

(a) not having enough time to study
(b) because she would risk failing
(c) she always gets good marks
(d) to switch from going jogging three times a week to playing football

21. Reading

(a) It stimulates your imagination / expands your mind.
(b) Learning new vocabulary.
(c) Young people are reading less than they used to due to technology.

22. Films

(a) exciting, (b) week

23. TV

(a) lively, (b) all ages, (c) Japan, (d) children aged 8–13

24. Celebrations

Sample answer

Para celebrar mi cumpleaños, me encanta hacer algo especial con mis amigos del instituto. Normalmente vamos al centro para ir al cine. La Navidad pasada, mi familia y yo fuimos a visitar a mis abuelos que viven en Estados Unidos. Pasamos unas vacaciones increíbles y me encantó jugar en la nieve antes de abrir los regalos. Las celebraciones son muy importantes porque unen a la gente y siempre son divertidas.

25. Festivals

Listen to the recording

SPEAKING TRACK 50

Sample answer

En esta foto se ve una fiesta tradicional con muchos fuegos artificiales magníficos. En la foto hay mucha gente y parece un espectáculo fantástico. A mí me encantaría ir a esta fiesta. Para mí las fiestas son muy importantes porque nos dan la oportunidad de entender más de la cultura de un lugar y formar parte de un grupo grande de gente de varias edades. Además, son muy divertidas. El año pasado mi familia y yo fuimos a una fiesta tradicional del pueblo pequeño donde vivo. Se cerraron las calles al tráfico y bailamos mucho. A mí me encantaría tener la oportunidad de ir a La Tomatina en España. Me parece una fiesta muy divertida y siempre he querido lanzar tomates a alguien.

Local area, holiday and travel

26. Holiday preferences

Sample answer

Mis vacaciones perfectas serían en Tailandia con un grupo de amigos del instituto. Podríamos hacer deportes acuáticos y bailar en algunas discotecas. Cuando estoy de vacaciones, lo

que no me gusta hacer es tomar el sol y descansar. Prefiero ser activo y aprender cosas nuevas. El año pasado, mi familia y yo fuimos a Francia para esquiar y fue fantástico. Me caí mucho el primer día pero fue muy divertido y al final de la semana había aprendido a esquiar en paralelo.

27. Hotels

Listen to the recording

SPEAKING TRACK 51

Sample answer:

C = candidate, T = teacher

T: Usted está en un hotel en España. Está hablando con el/la recepcionista. Quiere reservar una habitación.
T: Buenos días. ¿En qué puedo servirle?
C: Quiero una habitación doble con ducha, por favor.
T: Muy bien. ¿Para cuántas noches?
C: Me gustaría la habitación para cinco noches.
T: ¿Prefiere una habitación con vistas al mar o a la montaña?
C: Prefiero una habitación con vistas al mar.
T: De acuerdo. ¿Tiene planes para mañana?
C: Sí, vamos a visitar el castillo y luego nos gustaría ir a un restaurante típico.
T: ¿Tiene una pregunta?
C: ¿El desayuno está incluido en el precio de la habitación?
T: Sí, está incluido.

28. Camping

(a) the campsite
(b) the youth hostel

29. Accommodation

Listen to the recording

SPEAKING TRACK 52

Sample answer

En esta foto se ve una familia que está de vacaciones en un camping con su caravana. No me gusta nada pasar las vacaciones en un camping porque siempre es muy incómodo dormir en una tienda. Además, muchas veces los servicios están sucios o las duchas no funcionan. Normalmente voy a un camping bastante aburrido pero el año pasado me quedé en un hotel precioso de cinco estrellas. Tenía una piscina enorme y las habitaciones eran muy limpias y bastante grandes. Me encantan los hoteles lujosos pero el problema es que son muy caros. Mis vacaciones ideales serían en un país donde se hable español, como México, Cuba o Venezuela. Sé que estos países tienen unas playas hermosas y mucha cultura para conocer. Mi familia y yo pasaríamos quince días en un hotel bonito. Alquilaríamos bicicletas y nos bañaríamos en el mar cada mañana antes de desayunar. Comeríamos mucha fruta tropical y mariscos frescos. Lo pasaríamos genial.

31. Travelling

1 C, 2 B, 3 C

32. Holiday activities

Listen to the recording

SPEAKING TRACK 53

Sample answer

Siempre voy de vacaciones con mi hermana. Tiene dos años más que yo, por lo que tenemos los mismos gustos. El año pasado fuimos a Ibiza. ¡Fue estupendo! Nos bañamos en el mar y descansamos en la playa. Por las noches íbamos a las discotecas y bailábamos hasta las tres de la mañana. Yo creo que a mis padres les gustaría que fuéramos con ellos, pero sería aburrido.

33. Holiday experiences

(a) Everything was closed and there was nobody about.
(b) By bus or by bike.
(c) He tried to study and learn phrases to use with the family.
(d) 15

34. Transport and directions

(a) better for the environment
(b) catches the bus

35. Transport problems

(a) Alejandro, (b) Cristina, (c) Isabel, (d) Miguel, (e) Cristina

36. Holiday problems

(a) waiter is not doing job properly
(b) clean the tables / make sure everything is clean

37. Asking for help abroad

Sample answer
C = candidate, T = teacher
T: Usted está en una comisaría de España denunciando el robo de su monedero.
T: Buenas tardes. ¿Qué ha ocurrido exactamente?
C: Un hombre me ha robado el monedero hace media hora.
T: ¿Dónde ha tenido lugar el robo?
C: Tuvo lugar en el centro comercial, en un café.
T: ¿Puede describir al ladrón?
C: Sí. El ladrón era rubio con el pelo corto y rizado. Era bastante alto.
T: ¿Cómo es su monedero?
C: Es azul marino con rayas blancas.

38. Eating in a café

(a) María (c) Pablo (e) María
(b) Miguel (d) Miguel

39. Eating in a restaurant

(a) It's a great place where you can eat really well
   It's quiet.
(b) Colleagues from the office.
(c) Going somewhere else for coffee.
(d) No. There was nobody else there.
(e) It smelled of disinfectant.

40. Shopping for food

(a) D, (b) C, (c) A

41. Buying gifts

Sample answer
C = candidate, T = teacher

T: Usted está en una tienda de ropa en un pueblo de España y quiere comprar algo.
T: Hola. ¿En qué puedo ayudarle?
C: Me gustaría comprar una gorra.
T: Muy bien. Tenemos varios colores. ¿Cuál prefiere?
C: Prefiero una gorra roja.
T: Habla bien el español. ¿De dónde es usted?
C: Soy de Escocia.
T: Muy bien. ¿Le gusta este pueblo?
C: Sí, me gusta mucho porque es muy pintoresco y bastante pequeño.
T: ¿Tiene una pregunta?
C: ¿Cuánto es la gorra?
T: Son veinte euros.

42. Opinions about food

(a) Greek
(b) she doesn't have time
(c) very good and really tasty

43. The weather

(a) B, (b) A, (c) A

44. Places to see

(a) museum, (b) chemist's, (c) gallery, (d) bakery

45. Tourist information

… I found out lots of information, like/for example the bus timetable. Tomorrow I would like to do a walking tour through/around the town/city centre with my parents.

46. Describing a town

C, E, G

48. Places to visit

Sample answer
Se puede visitar el museo y así se conoce la cultura. A mí me encanta Bilbao porque se puede experimentar la cultura vasca. También se puede caminar por el casco antiguo y se puede ver un espectáculo de música vasca porque forma parte de su patrimonio cultural. ¿Usted ha visitado el casco antiguo de Bilbao?

49. Describing a region

(a) Tiene paisajes, pueblos blancos y costa.
(b) Hay (mucha) cultura y tradiciones.

School

50. School subjects

(a) Francisco (b) Francisco (c) Marcela (d) Francisco

51. School life

(a) No hablo nunca/Nunca hablo con mis amigos en clase.
(b) A veces leo libros en la biblioteca.
(c) Ayer por la mañana escribí un ensayo de historia.
(d) Prefiero hablar con el profesor/la profesora porque odio copiar de la pizarra.

52. The school day

(a) It only lasts 15 minutes.
(b) It lasts 45 minutes.
(c) He always has a club/activity (after school).

53. Comparing schools

 Listen to the recording

Sample answer
Los colegios en España son diferentes de los colegios ingleses. Los alumnos no llevan uniforme y en algunos colegios las clases terminan más tarde que en el mío. Las vacaciones son más largas: casi tres meses. ¡Me gustaría tener esas vacaciones en mi colegio!
En Inglaterra los alumnos llevan uniforme y no me gusta mucho, pero visité un instituto español durante un intercambio y ¡qué sorpresa! los alumnos españoles no tenían que llevarlo. ¡Qué envidia! ¡No es justo! Lo que no me da envidia es su horario. Los alumnos en el colegio que visité tienen clase hasta las cinco de la tarde. No me gustaría eso.

55. School rules

 Listen to the recording

Sample answer
En mi instituto tengo que llevar uniforme. Odio el uniforme porque es incómodo. En mi opinión, las normas son anticuadas. Son tontas e inútiles pero algunas personas piensan que son necesarias. ¡Qué horror!
En mi instituto, hay muchas normas. Acaban de introducir una nueva y ahora no se permite usar el móvil en clase. ¡No es justo! Hay que dejarlo en casa, o apagarlo antes de entrar en el instituto. Creo que los profesores son demasiado estrictos.

56. Problems at school

D, F

58. Success in school

(a) turn off your mobile
(b) doing homework well / concentrating in class
(c) patience / motivation / tenacity, persistence

59. School trips

(a) A, (b) C, (c) C

60. School events

(a) academic success / students going to universities / students continuing studying
(b) the play (they have just seen)
(c) the actors / those who helped during the show

61. School exchanges

 Listen to the recording

Sample answer
En esta foto hay un grupo de estudiantes ingleses que ha ido a España para hacer un intercambio. A mí me gustan mucho

los intercambios porque son emocionantes y te permiten aprender de otras culturas y costumbres. El año pasado hice un intercambio en Málaga, donde me quedé con una familia simpática. Comí muchos platos típicos y participé en tres excursiones a sitios históricos. En el futuro me encantaría volver a España para conocer otras regiones y ciudades. Viajaré en tren para disfrutar de los paisajes fascinantes. ¡Hay tanto que ver! A mi modo de ver, los intercambios son importantes porque nos ayudan a vivir una gran aventura y a dominar otros idiomas. Tienen beneficios incalculables para todos.

Future aspirations, study and work

62. Future plans

 Listen to the recording

Sample answer
Cuando sea mayor y termine la universidad, viajaré mucho. Ganaré mucho dinero así que seré feliz porque podré comprar mucha ropa.

64. Using languages

(a) (2 of:) travel to more than 20 countries / key in world of business / can understand your own language better and learn others more easily
(b) speak Spanish
(c) Chinese
(d) number of speakers will increase to 7.5% (by 2030)

65. Jobs

(a) firefighter
(b) he didn't like working at night
(c) waiter
(d) bricklayer / builder
(e) you can earn a lot of money

66. Opinions about jobs

(a) C, (b) D

67. Applying for jobs

B, E, F

68. Work experience

C, D, F

69. Volunteering

(a) communicating with others / improving personal relationships
(b) two years ago
(c) skills / better job prospects
(d) it was incredible / he'd recommend it

70. Helping others

(a) preparar una comida / ir al supermercado
(b) ofrecer hacer de canguro

71. Charities

(a) personas, (b) pobres, (c) colegios

72. Careers and training

Listen to the recording — SPEAKING TRACK 61

Sample answer
Como profesión tengo la idea de ser piloto porque me chiflan los aviones, me encanta volar y parece ser una profesión bastante variada. Creo que es esencial encontrar un trabajo bien pagado si quieres vivir en una ciudad como Londres.

73. Messages

(a) 667 78 96 78
(b) Iberia
(c) Monday to Friday, 9am–1pm
(d) 967 87 81 52

74. Part-time jobs

B, E, G

75. Money

(a) to buy a new mobile
(b) buy lots of magazines and books/novels
(c) she's going to work in a hairdresser's

International and global dimension

77. Music events

Listen to the recording — SPEAKING TRACK 62

Sample answer
C = candidate, T = teacher
T: Háblame de la foto.
C: En esta foto la gente está en un estadio escuchando un concierto de música rock. Hay muchos espectadores y el escenario es bastante grande.
T: A mí me gustan los eventos musicales. ¿Y a ti?
C: En realidad me encantan los eventos musicales porque cuando hay mucha gente, el ambiente es increíble.
T: Háblame de un concierto al que has asistido.
C: Mis amigos y yo fuimos a un concierto de nuestro grupo favorito. Bailamos mucho porque conocíamos todas las canciones. Fue una experiencia muy emocionante.
T: ¿Prefieres los eventos musicales o los eventos deportivos?
C: Por lo general prefiero los eventos musicales. A mi modo de ver son más divertidos porque el público participa más. La semana que viene iré a un concierto con mi novio y sé que cantaremos mucho.

78. Green issues

Listen to the recording — SPEAKING TRACK 63

Sample answer
Para mí, el problema más grande es el calentamiento global. Pienso que deberíamos usar más el transporte público y reutilizar más productos.

Es esencial que trabajemos contra la destrucción de la capa de ozono si queremos salvar nuestro planeta. Es necesario que reciclemos más y no deberíamos malgastar electricidad ni consumir tanta energía. Además, compraré pilas recargables y nunca más utilizaré bolsas de plástico.

79. Environmental action

Sample answer
Proteger el medio ambiente es esencial porque estamos destruyendo nuestro planeta. Creo que es muy importante reducir el uso de bolsas plásticas porque tardan años en descomponerse. Si más personas se pusieran a no usar bolsas plásticas, no habría tantos problemas de polución. También se puede viajar en bicicleta en vez de ir en autobús o coche. En el futuro, mi familia y yo vamos a reducir la energía que usamos porque nos ocupamos mucho del calentamiento global.

80. Global issues

A

81. Natural resources

(a) los ecosistemas terrestre, fluvial y marino
(b) que todos somos parte de la solución
(c) guardar los residuos y tirarlos en el contenedor adecuado

Grammar

82. Nouns and articles

1 (a) folletos   (c) tradiciones   (e) actores
   (b) veces   (d) cafés
2 (a) la, (b) el (c) el, (d) la, (e) la

83. Adjectives

pequeña, bonitas, internacionales, simpática, habladora, históricos, ruidosos, interesantes
Translation answer:
Mallorca is a small island. It has many beautiful beaches. In Mallorca there are lots of international tourists. People there are very kind and very talkative. Mallorca has lots of historical museums and a lot of noisy bars. You can do lots of interesting things.

84. Possessives and pronouns

mi, sus, mi, que, su, el mío, él, el suyo
Translation answer:
My stepfather is called Miguel. His daughters are my stepsisters. My stepsister, who is called Isabel, has a boyfriend, Pablo. Her boyfriend is less handsome than mine. I have been going out with him for six years. Isabel has been going out with hers for a month.

85. Comparisons

1 el peor   5 la mejor
2 los mejores   6 el más feo
3 la más bonita   7 más deportista
4 aburridísimo   8 más divertida

86. Other adjectives

1 Ese chico es mi primo.
2 Esta manzana está rica.
3 Quiero comprar esos vaqueros.
4 Aquella casa es grandísima.
5 Esta película es aburrida.
6 No quiero ese jersey – quiero aquella rebeca.

87. Pronouns

1 Voy a darlo a mi padre / Lo voy a dar a mi padre.
2 Le envío muchos mensajes.
3 Voy a comprarlo / Lo voy a comprar.
4 Ponlos en la bolsa.
5 Quiero decirle un secreto.

88. The present tense

1 escucho – I don't listen to classical music.
2 hablan – My parents speak English.
3 juega – My friend plays basketball with me.
4 quieres – Do you want to go to the cinema with me tonight?
5 comemos – We always eat fruit to be healthy.
6 encuentran – They always find money in the street.
7 vivís – Do you live in the countryside?
8 duerme – My brother sleeps in his own room.

89. Reflexive verbs (present)

1	Me	3	me	5	te
2	se	4	Nos	6	se

90. Irregular verbs (present)

1 salgo – I leave at 7.30 to go to the concert.
2 tienen – My cousins have blue eyes and they are blond.
3 sé – I really like to go/going to the beach but I don't know how to swim.
4 cojo – I always take the bus when I go to school.
5 hacen, hago – My friends do their homework in the library but I do it at home.
6 conduzco – I think that I drive very well but my father does not think so!

91. *Ser* and *estar*

1	está	3	es	5	son	7	están
2	es	4	estoy	6	es	8	está

92. The gerund

1 estoy / estaba jugando
2 estoy / estaba escribiendo
3 está / estaba hablando
4 está / estaba durmiendo
5 estoy / estaba comiendo
6 estoy / estaba tomando
7 están / estaban navegando
8 estás / estabas cantando

93. The preterite tense

1 I go to Italy. (present)
2 I arrived at six. (preterite)
3 I surf the internet. (present)
4 He / She listened to music. (preterite)
5 He / She went to a party which was great. (preterite)
6 It was cold and it rained a bit. (preterite)
7 We saw Pablo in the market. (preterite)
8 I played basketball on the beach. (preterite)

94. The imperfect tense

1	trabajaba	3	iba	5	visité
2	comí	4	había	6	lloraba

95. The future tense

1 (a) Nunca fumaré.
  (b) Ayudaré a los demás .
  (c) Cambiaremos el mundo.
  (d) Trabajaré en un aeropuerto.

2 (a) Voy a salir a las seis.
  (b) Voy a ser médico.
  (c) Va a ir a Pakistán.
  (d) Mañana voy a jugar al tenis.

96. The conditional tense

bebería, haría, practicaría, tomaría, bebería, comería, me acostaría, dormiría, llevaría

97. Perfect and pluperfect

1 He visitado Palma con mi novio. (perfect)
2 Han hecho sus deberes con mi ayuda. (perfect)
3 Habíamos ido al supermercado con Adel. (pluperfect)
4 Mi hermana ha escrito una carta de amor. (perfect)
5 ¿Has visto mi abrigo? (perfect)
6 Cuando llegó, mis primos habían comido ya. (pluperfect)

98. Giving instructions

1 Write to me.
2 Wait for your sister.
3 Don't tell me anything.
4 Don't shout!
5 Click here.
6 Don't take photos!
7 Answer the questions.
8 Don't leave everything to the last minute.

99. The present subjunctive

1 When I go to university, I'll study French.
2 I don't think your friend is good-looking.
3 When I'm 18, I'll take a gap year.
4 I want you to talk to Pablo.
5 It's not true that my clothes are horrible.
6 I don't think Italy is the best football team.

100. Negatives

Suggested answers:
1 No como nunca verduras.
2 No tengo ningún libro.
3 No conozco a nadie.
4 Nadie juega al baloncesto.
5 Nunca hago mis deberes.
6 No me gusta ni navegar por Internet ni descargar música.
7 No tiene nada.
8 No tengo ningún amigo en Londres.
Translation answers:
1 I always eat vegetables.
2 I have a book.
3 I know all (of) his / her friends.
4 Everyone plays basketball.
5 I always do my homework.
6 I like to surf the internet and download music.
7 It / He / She has everything.
8 I have lots of friends in London.

101. Special verbs

1	Me duele	5	Le duelen
2	Le gusta	6	Me encanta
3	Me gustaron	7	Nos quedan
4	Les hace falta	8	A María le gustan

102. *Por* and *para*

1 (a) para, (b) para, (c) por, (d) para, (e) para, (f) por, (g) por
2 (a) para, (b) por, (c) para, (d) por, (e) ✓, (f) para, (g) ✓, (h) ✓

103. Questions and exclamations

1	d	**3**	h	**5**	a	**7**	c
2	f	**4**	e	**6**	b	**8**	g

104. Connectives and adverbs

1 *Suggested answers*:
  (a) Nunca voy al teatro porque es aburrido.
  (b) Mientras jugaba al baloncesto, Juan hacía patinaje.
  (c) Después de estudiar, iré a la universidad.
  (d) Nos gustaría ir a la playa pero está lloviendo.
2 (a) tranquilamente (peacefully)
  (b) perfectamente (perfectly)
  (c) difícilmente (with difficulty)
  (d) severamente (strictly)

105. Numbers

1 las nueve menos veinte
2 cuatrocientos sesenta y cinco
3 el doce de junio de dos mil catorce
4 séptimo
5 las once y media
6 setenta y seis
7 el primero / el uno de enero de mil novecientos noventa y siete
8 tercero

Vocabulary

117. Internet and social media

1 Me gusta chatear en línea con mis amigos por la tarde.
2 El ciberacoso no es un problema en mi instituto.
3 Quiero ser programador cuando deje el instituto.

Published by Pearson Education Limited, 80 Strand, London, WC2R 0RL.

www.pearsonschoolsandfecolleges.co.uk

Copies of official specifications for all Pearson qualifications may be found on the website: qualifications.pearson.com

Text, audio and illustrations © Pearson Education Limited 2017, 2021
Typeset and illustrated by Kamae Design, Oxford and Newgen Knowledgeworks
Produced by Cambridge Publishing Management Ltd and Newgen Publishing UK
Cover illustration by Kamae Design Ltd

The right of Leanda Reeves to be identified as author of this work has been asserted by her in accordance with the Copyright, Designs and Patents Act 1988.

First published 2021

24

10 9 8 7

British Library Cataloguing in Publication Data
A catalogue record for this book is available from the British Library
ISBN 9781292412221

Printed and bound by CPI Group (UK) Ltd, Croydon, CR0 4YY

Acknowledgements
Content written by Ian Kendrick and Vivien Halksworth is included.

The publisher would like to thank the following for their kind permission to reproduce their photographs:

123RF: Jaysi 29c, Cathy Yeulet 58c, Sanchai Khudpin 60cl; **Alamy Stock Photo:** PERRONE CLAUDIO/NEWZULU/CrowdSpark 9cl, Lucas Vallecillos 21cl, Eddie Gerald 25c, Pixoi Ltd 66cl, Neil Juggins 79cr, Adrian Weinbrecht/Image Source 81c; **Getty Images:** IStock 53cl, PhotoAlto/Frederic Cirou/PhotoAlto Agency RF Collections 81cr; Carol Yepes/ Moment 84br; **Pearson Education Ltd:** Sophie Bluy 4cr, 18cl; Tudor Photography 41cr; Studio 8 83br, 87br, MindStudio 84c, 85cr; **Shutterstock:** Shutterstock 5cl, Stock Studio 35cr, Sea Wave 38cr, Shutterstock 39cr, By Kapitula Olga 41c, PhotoBarmaley 45cr, Michiru13 47, Julinzy 47c, Roihunmatpor 47 (2), Globe Turner 47, Aueng Indy 55c, Jan kranendonk 61cr, Shutterstock 61b, Grafvision 63c, Rawpixel.com 65tr, Helder Almeida 66cr, Fizkes 67cl, Shutterstock 72c, 73tr, Minerva Studio 74cr, Goran Djukanovic 77c, Hurst Photo 78cr, Pixel Shot 79tr, Tana888 80cl, Fedor Selivanov 81tr, Rawpixel.com 84l, Shutterstock 86br, Prostock studio 86tr, RamonaS 91c, Fizkes 91bc, Joshua Haviv 93tr, Darren Baker 95cr, Moloko88 96bl, Prostock studio 102c, Debr22pics 102cr.

All other images © Pearson Education

We are grateful to the following for permission to reproduce copyright material:

Page 20: **Editorial Destino:** Extract from *Sara y las Goleadoras 6: El último gol* © Laura Gallego García, Editorial Destino, 2010; Page 33: **Anaya Infantil y Juvenil:** Extract from *Donde aprenden a volar las gaviotas* by Ana Alcolea. Anaya Infantil y Juvenil, 2007; Page 39: **Ediciones Siruela SA:** Extract from *Una Madre* by Alejandro Palomas. Ediciones Siruela, 2014; Page 71: **Save the Children Spain:** Extract adapted from Save the Children Spain Mission Statement: https://www.savethechildren.es/trabajo-ong/pobreza-infantil/pobreza-infantil-en-espana Accessed: January 2017 © Save the Children, 2017; Logo © Save the Children, 2017; Page 80: **LibrosEnRed:** Extract from Los valores y sus desafios by Jose Ramon Fabelo Corzo. Libros en Red, 2004; Page 81: **PROYECTO LIBERA/ECOEMBES:** Extract from Campaña por el medio ambiente "Reflexiones". Proyecto LIBERA: SEO/BIRDLIFE & ECOEMBES (2018). https://www.ecoembes.com/es/ciudadanos/sala-de-prensa/notas-de-prensa/campana-por-el-medio-ambiente-reflexiones Accessed: 18 Aug 2021.